# 40 HADITH FROM

# Sunan ibn Majah

## SHAHRUL HUSSAIN
## & ZAHED FETTAH

*Forty Hadith from Sunan Ibn Mājah*

First Published in 2023 by
THE ISLAMIC FOUNDATION

*Distributed by*
KUBE PUBLISHING LTD
Tel +44 (0)1530 249230
E-mail: info@kubepublishing.com
Website: www.kubepublishing.com

*Author* Shahrul Hussain *&* Zahed Fettah
*Editor* Umm Marwan Ibrahim
*Cover Design* Afreen Fazil (Jaryah Studios)
*Arabic/English layout & design* Nasir Cadir

A Cataloguing-in-Publication Data record for this book
is available from the British Library

ISBN 978-0-86037-985-0
eISBN 978-0-86037-990-4

Printed by Elma Basim, Turkey

# Dedication

*For Liyana and Leena*

ॐ

# *Contents*

# *Introduction*

All praise is due to Allah, the Lord of the universe, the Most
Merciful the Most Kind, the Master of the Day of Judgement.
Peace and blessings be upon Muhammad ﷺ, the final Prophet of
Allah, and upon his family and Companions.

Hadith is one of the most important institutions in Islam. It contains
the teachings of the Prophet Muhammad ﷺ regarding all aspects of
Islam. It is indispensable in order to attain the correct understanding
of the religion, and without it, guidance is not possible. Therefore, it
is essential for all Muslims to make an effort to understand and study
Hadith, even if it is at a basic level.

Unfortunately, most of the works of Hadith literature available in
English are long, detailed, and viewed as heavy reads by the general
masses. As these are religious texts, it can be daunting for beginners
to understand the subject. There are mainly two types of books about
Hadith in English. While one type deals with the science of Hadith
in terms of its historical phenomena as a vital Islamic institution,
the other consists of thick volumes of English renditions of Hadith
corpuses—both of which can put off beginners from reading and
understanding Hadith.

This dilemma gave birth to the 'Forty Ahadith' project, in which we set out to compile a series of forty ahadith from each of the six canonical books of Hadith. The collection aims to educate people who wish to enjoy Hadith literature without delving too deep into its technicalities. The style and language used in these books is non-specialised and thereby accessible to readers of all levels and ages. As such, the collection is also ideal for new Muslims who wish to learn more about Hadith.

In this volume, we have selected forty ahadith from *Sunan Ibn Mājah* in order to give the reader a flavour of the Hadith literature found within the *Sunan*. There is no particular reason for choosing the ahadith mentioned herein. However, each hadith will reflect a unique theme so as to touch upon various aspects of the Islamic teachings, such as:

- Manners and Etiquettes
- Character of a Muslim
- Exhortations and Admonitions
- Remembrance of Allah
- Knowledge and Action
- Beliefs

When selecting the forty ahadith for each book in the series, we made sure to avoid lengthy and elaborate narrations or those that dealt with complex legal and theological matters. Instead, you will find that the selected ahadith focus on character, spirituality, morals, manners and ethics, and that the accompanying explanations of the ahadith focus on highlighting these aspects.

Within this volume is a simple discussion of the theoretical parameters of praiseworthy characters every Muslim should aspire to achieve, supererogatory virtuous acts of worship, and the moral philosophy (in particular normative ethics) of these ahadith. It is hoped that this will open the doors for readers to enquire more about Hadith as an important source of revelation.

Finally, it is worth pointing out that the reason for compiling forty ahadith is due to the virtuous nature of 'forty' ahadith recorded in many traditions of the Prophet Muhammad ﷺ. It is related that Prophet Muhammad ﷺ said, 'Whoever memorises forty ahadith regarding the matters of religion, Allah will resurrect him on the Day of Judgement from among the group of jurists and scholars' (*Bayhaqī*). Although this hadith is weak in its authenticity, many scholars have strongly supported acting on weak ahadith, which solely speak about virtues of good deeds, for the sake of spirituality. What is of even more benefit is to memorise forty ahadith from *Sunan Ibn Mājah*. The short ahadith in this compilation may help facilitate young learners and beginners to memorise the beloved Prophet's sayings, which would be a great achievement.

We would like to conclude by thanking everyone who has made this project possible, especially Br Haris Ahmad from Kube Publishing Ltd for his support; without his help, this project would not have been possible. The people we are most indebted to are the patrons of the Ibn Rushd Centre of Excellence for Islamic Research. This work is dedicated to them and all those who support the advancement of knowledge and research.

**Shahrul Hussain** *&* **Zahed Fettah**
8th April 2019 / 3rd Sha'bān 1440

# *Acknowledgments*

It would not be possible to accomplish this work without the support of many great people, too many to mention all of them by name. First and foremost, we thank our parents for their love and support. Our teachers without whom we would be nothing.

We are most obliged to mention our heartfelt thanks to all the editors for their invaluable feedback. The English language or indeed any other language does not afford a word to express our deepest gratitude to Br Rizvan Khalid for his support and help. We would like to thank Dr Ahmed al-Dubayan, General Director of the Islamic Cultural Centre for his support and friendship, and for his kind words of encouragement.

Special thanks to my students Shaykh Morshed Alam and Moulana Mohummed Yoosuf Zaaman for the commitment and dedication.

*"I ask Allah to raise the rank of my parents and bless them in this life and the next, for they have encouraged me on my path of learning and seeking knowledge."*

Zahed Fettah

# *A Brief Biography of Imam Ibn Mājah*

Imam Ibn Mājah is (Abū 'Abdullāh) Muḥammad ibn Yazīd al-Qazwīnī. He was born in the year 209 AH in Qazwīn (Qazvin); a city in the north of what is known today as Iran. Like all the scholars of Hadith of his time, he travelled to many parts of the world to study and narrate ahadith. His journey to seek ahadith took him to Makkah, Basra, Kufa, Baghdad, Sham (Levant), Egypt, and elsewhere. These places were considered the leading centres of Hadith at the time.

Imam Ibn Mājah studied and narrated ahadith from some of the greatest Hadith scholars of his time. Some of the most prominent of them include Abū Bakr ibn Abī Shaybah, Abū Khaythamah Zuhayr ibn Ḥarb, and Muḥammad ibn Yaḥyā al-Dhuhlī, the imam of Ahl al-Hadith in Nishapur. Some scholars have compiled a list of the teachers whom Imam Ibn Mājah narrated ahadith from, and they reached over 300 from different parts of the world. Ibn Khallikān said about Imam Ibn Mājah: 'He was an imam (leading scholar) in Hadith. He was knowledgeable in all its sciences and all that which relates to Hadith.'

One of his key students was Abū al-Ḥasan 'Alī ibn Ibrāhīm al-Qaṭṭān (d. 345 AH). His importance stems from the fact that he narrated *Sunan Ibn Mājah* from the author towards the end of the author's life, making his narration of the book the most relied upon today. Al-Qaṭṭān was no more than 20 years of age when he narrated the book from his teacher and lived for around 70 years after the passing of his teacher. The scholars mentioned that Imam Ibn Mājah also authored other books including works on *tafsīr* and history. Imam Ibn Kathīr said: 'He has an incredible *tafsīr* (explanation of the Qur'an) and a complete historical work from the time of the Companions until his time.' These indicate that he was a man of vast knowledge of the Qur'an, Hadith and history. However, it is his book the *Sunan* which became known and continues to play an important role until this day. The other two books unfortunately have been lost, although some scholars of the previous centuries had come across them.

Imam Ibn Mājah was highly praised by the scholars for his vast knowledge, particularly in the sciences of Hadith. His book, today known as *Sunan Ibn Mājah*, is amongst the six principal references of Hadith today. It is a book that contains just over 4,000 Hadith on most of the topics of Islam. The book is a clear sign of the author's knowledge; and hence, it is from the books which continue to be studied and narrated in Hadith circles until this day. However, unlike the other six books, the comments of the author in his book or elsewhere are limited. There is little reported from him regarding the authenticity of reports, hadith defects and hadith narrators, but his chapter headings are useful.

Imam Ibn Mājah died in the year 273 AH. May Allah have mercy on him.

## The Importance of Hadith and its Significance

Allah sent Messengers throughout history with the objective of clarifying the truth to the people and guiding them to Him. Many of these Messengers were also sent with Books containing guidance, such as the final Messenger of Allah, Prophet Muhammad ﷺ. He was sent to teach the Book, the Qur'an, and to be the living example of the teachings of the Qur'an. As Allah states in the Qur'an: *'Allah has surely conferred a favour on the believers when He sent in their midst a Messenger from among themselves who recites to them His verses, purifies them, and teaches them the Book and the Wisdom, while previously they had been in clear misguidance'* (*Āl 'Imrān* 3: 164). Allah also states: *'And we have sent down the Reminder (the Qur'an) to you so that you (O Messenger) may clarify to the people that which has been sent down to them, and so that they may ponder'* (*al-Naḥl* 16: 44).

These verses highlight that the role of the Messenger ﷺ is to clarify and teach the Qur'an. His words and his actions, which form a verbal and practical interpretation of the Qur'an, is the Prophetic Tradition referred to as the 'Sunnah'. Following the Sunnah is necessary because it is the only way to practice the teachings of the final Book of Allah correctly.

Allah has taken it upon Himself to preserve the Qur'an: *'It is certainly We who have revealed the Reminder, and it is certainly We who will preserve it'* (*al-Ḥijr* 15: 9). This preservation is not restricted to the letters and words of the Qur'an but also includes the preservation of its meanings, which is fulfilled through the Prophetic implementation of the Qur'an—the Sunnah.

It is simply not possible to observe the teachings of Islam without following the Sunnah. The purpose of the Qur'an is to teach us the correct belief and acts of worship Allah demands from us in order to prove our servitude to Him. It is not, however, an instruction manual detailing precise rules and methods of worshipping Allah.

Moreover, written or verbal instructions are not enough; it requires a teacher to show us the practical way of worshipping Allah. Thus, while the Qur'an outlines the commandments of Allah such as to fast, give zakat, perform hajj and the like, the role of the Prophet ﷺ is to teach us *how* to perform those acts of worship. Therefore, without knowing and following the Sunnah, Muslims will not be able to observe the teachings of the Qur'an.

## Compilation of Hadith

Although the Qur'an was collected and written in one place much earlier than the Hadith, the latter was also preserved in similar ways to the former. Ahadith were written down by some Companions at the time of the Messenger 🕮, but this habit only became widespread a century or so after his death.

Since the second century after *hijrah*, many scholars wrote down the ahadith of the Prophet 🕮. Some scholars compiled books of Hadith which discussed the various areas of the teachings of the Prophet 🕮. Sadly, some of the earliest books of Hadith were lost. However, some survived and were transmitted throughout centuries until our time, including the *Muwaṭṭā'* of Imam Mālik (d. 179 AH), the *Muṣannaf* of 'Abd al-Razzāq (d. 211 AH), the *Muṣannaf* of Ibn Abī Shaybah (d. 235 AH), and the *Musnad* of Imam Aḥmad ibn Ḥanbal (d. 241 AH). These books contain thousands of reports from the Prophet 🕮 and his Companions, clarifying how they implemented the Qur'anic teachings in their everyday life.

Hundreds of books of Hadith were authored, but only a dozen of them became famous and spread worldwide. The nine most relied-upon books of Hadith are:

1. *Ṣaḥīḥ al-Bukhārī*
2. *Ṣaḥīḥ Muslim*
3. *Sunan Abū Dāwūd*
4. *Sunan al-Tirmidhī*
5. *Sunan al-Nasā'ī*
6. *Sunan Ibn Mājah*
7. *Muwaṭṭa' Mālik*
8. *Musnad Aḥmad*
9. *Musnad al-Dārimī*

## The Classification of Hadith

In the early generations, during the time of the Companions of the Prophet, it was quite easy to know the Sunnah of the Prophet ﷺ because the Companions had witnessed him directly. Unfortunately, in the generations that followed, some people would make false attributions to the Prophet ﷺ and claim that he said things which he had not said. They would do this with different intentions and agendas. This led to the scholars of Hadith putting an impressive amount of effort into preserving the Sunnah and distinguishing between authentic reports and false ones. They would study chains of narrations, the biographies of hadith narrators, and the texts of hadith in order to conclude which reports can comfortably be attributed to the Prophet ﷺ. Volumes have been written about those who narrated hadith so that we are able to know who the reliable and unreliable transmitters of hadith are. This effort was a collective one by many of the greatest scholars of Hadith, ensuring that the Sunnah of the Prophet ﷺ was preserved so that the Muslims may act upon it as Allah commanded them in the Qur'an.

This effort to study the Prophetic Traditions resulted in the formation of the science of Hadith. This became one of the most important of the Islamic sciences. It discusses chains of narration, different types of ahadith, the conditions for an authentic hadith, the different methods of transmitting hadith, the *fiqh* (understanding) of ahadith, and other relevant areas. Separate books have been authored in this science, known as *uṣūl al-ḥadīth* or *muṣṭalaḥ al-ḥadīth*, from the fourth century onwards. Some prominent works in this field include, *Maʿrifat ʿUlūm al-Ḥadīth* by Ḥākim al-Naysābūrī (d. 405 AH) and *Maʿrifat Anwāʿ ʿUlūm al-Ḥadīth* by Imam Abū ʿAmr ibn al-Ṣalāḥ (d. 643 AH).

Studying the sciences of Hadith is an essential part of Islamic studies. We can only understand the Qur'an and the Shariah if we have a strong grounding in the sciences of Hadith and a good understanding of the *fiqh* of Hadith.

However, Hadith studies is usually a subject for the most dedicated of learners because it requires attention to detail. For instance, there are many classifications and categories of Hadith. Advanced readers can refer to the *Muqaddimah* by Ibn Ṣalāḥ which is also available in English. Readers who have access to Arabic can refer to many resources such as *al-Irshād* by al-Nawawī (which he later summarised in his *Taqrīb*), al-Suyūṭī's *Tadrīb al-Rāwī*, Ibn Kathīr's *Ikhtiṣār 'Ulūm al-Ḥadīth*, al-Zarkashī's *al-Nukat*, al-'Iraqī's *al-Taqyīd wa al-Īḍāḥ* and Ibn Ḥajar al-'Asqalānī's *Nukhbat al-Fikr*.

As a beginner, you should know that scholars have made four major classifications of hadith based on the soundness of the hadith in terms of the reliability and memory of its reporters:

1. *Ṣaḥīḥ* (rigorously authentic)
2. *Ḥasan* (good)
3. *Ḍa'īf* (weak)
4. *Mawḍū'* (fabricated)

### *Ṣaḥīḥ* (rigorously authentic)

This is defined by Ibn Ṣalāḥ as a hadith which has a continuous chain of narrators (*isnād*), who have narrated the hadith from only trustworthy (*thiqah*) narrators (those with perfect memory and uprightness) and it (the hadith) is free from irregularities (in the text) and defects (in the *isnād*). Such as: Mālik—from Nāfi'—from 'Abdullāh ibn Umar.

### *Ḥasan* (good)

Al-Tirmidhī defines *ḥasan* as a hadith which is not irregular (*shādh*) nor contains a disparaged reporter in its chain of narrators, and is reported through more than one channel. Examples of *ḥasan* ahadith are those which have been reported by: 'Amr ibn Shu'ayb—from his father—from his grandfather or Muḥammad ibn 'Amr—from Abū

Salamah—from Abū Hurayrah.

## *Ḍaʿīf* (weak)

A weak hadith is a hadith which has failed to meet the standard of *ṣaḥīḥ* or *ḥasan*. It is usually one that has faults in the continuity of the chain of narrators (*isnād*) or has a fault in a narrator in terms of lack of reliability either in memory or uprightness.

## *Mawḍūʿ* (fabricated)

These are ahadith which the Prophet Muhammad ﷺ never said, but due to personal motives, were fabricated and attributed to him. A fabricated hadith can be detected either because one of the narrators is known to be a liar or because the text is of an obnoxious nature, thus going against the principles of Islam. For example, it is (falsely) attributed to the Prophet Muhammad ﷺ that he said, 'A negro will fornicate when his belly is full and steal when he is hungry.' This is fabricated due to its obnoxious nature, hence going against the noble character of the Prophet Muhammad ﷺ.

Oftentimes though, the wordings of a fabricated hadith may be non-offensive or even sound sensible. For example, 'To return one *dāniq* (a sixth of a dirham) to its owner is better than worshipping (Allah) for seventy years.' At such instances, scrutinising the hadith based on the thoroughly developed science of hadith classification would help us determine if it was in fact narrated by the Prophet Muhammad ﷺ or simply made up and falsely attributed to him.

# Absence of Scholars: A Sign of the Day of Judgement

عَنْ عَمْرِو بْنِ شُعَيْبٍ عَنْ أَبِيهِ قَالَ قَامَ مُعَاوِيَةُ خَطِيبًا فَقَالَ أَيْنَ عُلَمَاؤُكُمْ أَيْنَ عُلَمَاؤُكُمْ سَمِعْتُ رَسُولَ اللهِ ﷺ يَقُولُ لاَ تَقُومُ السَّاعَةُ إِلاَّ وَطَائِفَةٌ مِنْ أُمَّتِي ظَاهِرُونَ عَلَى النَّاسِ لاَ يُبَالُونَ مَنْ خَذَلَهُمْ وَلاَ مَنْ نَصَرَهُمْ

'Amr ibn Shu'ayb narrated that his father said: 'Mu'awiyah stood up to deliver a sermon and said: "Where are your scholars? Where are your scholars? For I heard the Messenger of Allah ﷺ say: 'The Hour will not begin until a group of my followers (*ummah*) will prevail over the people, and they will not care who lets them down and who supports them.'"'

There are many trials that we face in this life. One of the greatest of these trials is the trial of falsehood. If one is not careful, one can easily be led astray and follow falsehood. We are therefore required to put effort into remaining on the path of guidance and avoiding the path of misguidance. With so much information and so many opinions, how do we know what is right and what is false? It is the role of the righteous scholars who follow the Qur'an and Sunnah strictly to help explain what is right and what is false.

In this hadith, the Prophet Muhammad ﷺ told us that there will always be a group of brave people from the Muslims sticking firmly to the truth. They will not be harmed by the fact that most people are not with them, because the truth is not necessarily always with the majority. While most people's lives are directed by decisions based on desires, ignorance and following the crowd, few are those who are willing to think and ponder, even if that requires them to oppose the mainstream views around them. Despite the confusion that will only become more severe with time, there will always be a group of people who remain upon the truth. Imam al-Bukhārī said that these people are the people of knowledge—*the scholars*. They will stick firmly to the revelation of Allah and the path of His Prophet. They will therefore be able to distinguish between truth and falsehood, and keep themselves protected from going astray.

Remaining upon the truth can only be done by understanding and following the Sunnah, and by following those scholars who are well-versed in and live by the Prophetic teachings. By the Grace of Allah, the majority of Muslims are upon the truth, because they follow the main teachings of Islam, such as the five pillars of Islam, the six pillars of faith, and abstaining from the major sins. However, confusion and chaos exist, and they continue to increase. In these situations, it is all the more necessary to keep to the Sunnah and consult the scholars who have deep knowledge of the Qur'an and Sunnah.

This hadith is a warning against the absence of scholars and therefore it is an indirect message that the Muslim community must sponsor and fund students to learn and train to be scholars. If they fail to do that, they will fail to understand the religion of Allah correctly.

৩৯৩

# Poverty and Luxury

عَنْ أَبِى الدَّرْدَاءِ قَالَ خَرَجَ عَلَيْنَا رَسُولُ اللهِ ﷺ وَنَحْنُ نَذْكُرُ الْفَقْرَ
وَنَتَخَوَّفُهُ فَقَالَ آلْفَقْرَ تَخَافُونَ وَالَّذِى نَفْسِى بِيَدِهِ لَتُصَبَّنَّ
عَلَيْكُمُ الدُّنْيَا صَبًّا حَتَّى لاَ يُزِيغَ قَلْبَ أَحَدٍ مِنْكُمْ إِزَاغَةً إِلاَّ
هِيَهْ وَايْمُ اللهِ لَقَدْ تَرَكْتُكُمْ عَلَى مِثْلِ الْبَيْضَاءِ لَيْلُهَا وَنَهَارُهَا
سَوَاءٌ ۞ قَالَ أَبُو الدَّرْدَاءِ صَدَقَ وَاللهِ رَسُولُ اللهِ ﷺ تَرَكَنَا وَاللهِ عَلَى
مِثْلِ الْبَيْضَاءِ لَيْلُهَا وَنَهَارُهَا سَوَاءٌ

Abū al-Dardā' ؓ said: 'The Messenger of Allah ﷺ came
out to us when we were speaking of poverty and how we
feared it. He said: "Is it poverty that you fear? By the One
in whose Hand is my soul, [the delights and luxuries of]
this world will come to you in plenty, and nothing will
cause your hearts to deviate except that. By Allah, I am

leaving you upon something like *Bayḍā'* (a white, bright, and clear path) the night and day of which are the same.'"

Allah describes the Prophet Muhammad ﷺ in the Qur'an as being a warner. He was someone who warned us of all the things which harm us in this life and will result in disgrace in the afterlife. We must learn and take seriously what the Prophet ﷺ warned against, because he spoke with guidance and revelation from Allah. In another hadith reported by al-Bukhārī and Muslim, the Prophet Muhammad ﷺ said, 'By Allah, it is not poverty that I fear for you, but I am afraid that you will lead a life of luxury as past nations did, whereupon you will compete with each other for it, as they competed for it, and it will destroy you as it destroyed them.' This hadith clarifies why wealth and luxury can be a dangerous thing. Humans are naturally inclined towards money and worldly pleasures. If they allow this inclination to overtake their hearts, they will give it more importance than anything else. They would be willing to commit sin, cut ties of kinship, and oppress, for the sake of these worldly pleasures.

To help overcome the trials of this life, the Prophet ﷺ has left for us a 'clear bright path'. It is easy to understand and can easily be followed if we rely upon Allah to make this path easy for us. This path puts everything into its right place, teaching us how to balance between the duties of this life and its pleasures. This beautiful path that we have been blessed with teaches us that wealth and worldly pleasures have their place in our lives, so long as we can keep ourselves in check. It is our duty to study the teachings of the Prophet ﷺ and implement them in our lives, so that we can keep the necessary balance which brings us success in this life and the Hereafter. This hadith also teaches us that the nature of the Qur'an and Sunnah is one of ease and simplicity; easy to understand and easy to practice. The duty of the teachers of Islam is thus to understand it well and present it in an easy and clear manner.

# The Importance of the Sunnah

عَنْ عُبَيْدِ اللَّهِ بْنِ أَبِى رَافِعٍ عَنْ أَبِيهِ أَنَّ رَسُولَ اللَّهِ ﷺ قَالَ لاَ أُلْفِيَنَّ أَحَدَكُمْ مُتَّكِئًا عَلَى أَرِيكَتِهِ يَأْتِيهِ الأَمْرُ مِمَّا أَمَرْتُ بِهِ أَوْ نَهَيْتُ عَنْهُ فَيَقُولُ لاَ أَدْرِى مَا وَجَدْنَا فِي كِتَابِ اللَّهِ اتَّبَعْنَاهُ

It was narrated from 'Ubaydullāh ibn Abī Rāfi' from his father that the Messenger of Allah ﷺ said: 'I do not want to find anyone of you reclining on his pillow, and when news comes to him of something that I have commanded or forbidden, he says, I do not know, we will [only] follow what we find in the Book of Allah.'

The teachings of the Prophet Muhammad ﷺ are our greatest form of guidance. This is because the Prophet ﷺ showed us how to live by the Qur'an. His Sunnah is a practical embodiment of the Qur'an. The person who does not follow the Sunnah is not following the Qur'an correctly, because the Prophet ﷺ was sent to teach us the proper understanding of the Qur'an. Allah commands in the Qur'an: *'We have not sent before you a Messenger except that he should be obeyed by the permission of Allah'* (*al-Nisā'* 4: 64). Allah also says: *'So let those who disobey his [the Prophet's] orders beware, for an affliction may befall them, or a painful torment may overtake them'* (*al-Nūr* 24: 63). These are only two examples from amongst tens of verses in the Qur'an in which we are commanded to follow and obey the Prophet ﷺ. Following the Sunnah is therefore part of following the Qur'an. To not follow the Sunnah would be an act of disobedience to Allah's commands in the Qur'an.

The Qur'an often contains the commandments of Allah without detail, and it was the duty of the Prophet Muhammad ﷺ to teach his followers how these commandments are supposed to be executed. Therefore, through this hadith, the Prophet ﷺ taught Muslims that it is not sufficient to follow the Qur'an without his Sunnah. In other words, there is no guidance without following the Sunnah. In this hadith, the Prophet ﷺ also warned his followers that there will be people who will claim to only follow the Qur'an and they will refuse to follow anything that is reported to them from the Prophet ﷺ even if it is from trusted sources. This is something which we unfortunately see today. Some people believe that they can follow the Qur'an without knowing the teachings of the Prophet ﷺ. This is certainly not possible.

For instance, the Qur'an does not detail the method of prayer or hajj. One is thus unable to follow the commands of the Qur'an about prayer or hajj, except through the Prophetic teachings. Allah has favoured the Muslims by ensuring that hundreds of Hadith scholars worked hard to preserve the Sunnah. They, in turn, ensured that anything which is incorrectly attributed to the Prophet ﷺ is pointed out and anything which is authentically attributed through trusted individuals is preserved and followed. This has made it easy for us to understand the Qur'an and live by it.

This hadith also teaches us the importance of learning about the Sunnah and making an effort to understand the Qur'an. A person who does this would realise the importance and necessity of following the Prophet's teachings and how it is connected to the Qur'an.

# The Environment: Removing Harm from the Roads

عَنْ أَبِي بَرْزَةَ الأَسْلَمِيِّ قَالَ قُلْتُ يَا رَسُولَ اللَّهِ دُلَّنِي عَلَى عَمَلٍ
أَنْتَفِعُ بِهِ قَالَ اعْزِلِ الأَذَى عَنْ طَرِيقِ الْمُسْلِمِينَ

It was narrated that Abū Barzah al-Aslamī ﷺ said: 'O Messenger of Allah! Tell me of an action by which I may benefit.' He said: 'Remove harmful things from the path of the Muslims.'

What makes the Prophet's Companions special is their love to always better themselves. Beyond the compulsory duties, they would always ask the Prophet Muhammad ﷺ how they could better themselves. The Prophet ﷺ would look at any shortcoming they had and advised them to focus on that particular aspect. For example, a man came to the Prophet Muhammad ﷺ and asked him for advice on how to better himself. The Prophet ﷺ knew that the questioner had issues with his temper; so he advised him not to get angry.[1] The Prophet ﷺ knew that if he were to address his temper problem, a lot of his other problems would be automatically resolved. That is why the Prophet ﷺ repeatedly told the man to control his temper despite the man's request for further advice.

In this hadith, it is related that Abū Barzah al-Aslamī once came to the Prophet Muhammad ﷺ and asked him for advice about doing voluntary deeds which will be of great benefit. The Prophet ﷺ told him to remove anything from the path which is harmful for people. What harms people can differ from society to society and place to place. Litter may not sound like a major issue in many societies, but for some it is a major concern. Islam teaches us to keep clean. Therefore, not only is it rewardable to pick up litter, but it is also rewardable to bin the litter and not throw it on the floor. This applies to fly-tipping and any other social nuisances.

Although the hadith says the 'path of Muslims', it does not mean to restrict it to Muslims, while ignoring the roads of non-Muslims. Rather, this was said in a particular context and perhaps meant to give special emphasis to taking care of our brothers and sisters, while also taking care of those who are not Muslims. This is because Islam promotes the well-being of everyone in society. This is why everyone has a duty to look after their neighbours regardless of their faith.

This hadith can also be applied to actions that can harm the environment and stopping any harm to it. The aim of the hadith was not only to keep roads clean but to rid society of harm generally. Therefore, any type of harm is wrong, and doing everything possible to stop harm is a duty and a great act of worship.

〄

---

1    Al-Bukhari, *Sahih al-Bukhari*, Hadith no. 1492

# The Ruling on Wearing Silk and Gold

عَنْ عَبْدِ اللَّهِ بْنِ عَمْرٍو قَالَ خَرَجَ عَلَيْنَا رَسُولُ اللَّهِ ﷺ وَفِي إِحْدَى يَدَيْهِ ثَوْبٌ مِنْ حَرِيرٍ وَفِي الْأُخْرَى ذَهَبٌ فَقَالَ إِنَّ هَذَيْنِ مُحَرَّمٌ عَلَى ذُكُورِ أُمَّتِي حِلٌّ لِإِنَاثِهِمْ

'Abdullāh ibn 'Umar ﷺ said: 'The Messenger of Allah ﷺ came out to us, and in one of his hands was a garment of silk and in the other was some gold. He said: "These are forbidden for the males of my nation and permitted for the females.'"

The general rule is that all guidance revealed in the Qur'an and through the teachings of the Prophet ﷺ are for men and women. However, due to some differences that exist between men and women, there are some rulings which are applicable only to men and others only to women. Men and women bring an essential balance to societies. When the lines between the two genders are blurred, it will create a dangerous imbalance for the upbringing of children, the family, community, and wider society. For this reason, Islam has prohibited imitating the opposite gender to ensure that men maintain their masculinity and that women maintain their femininity. All people love to uphold a beautiful appearance and wear presentable clothes, and this is encouraged even in the Qur'an. However, there are some restrictions to this, especially for men, to ensure that there is not an excessive focus on their appearance.

More scope is given for women to wear jewellery and to dress as they like, because this is consistent with their feminine nature. For men, on the other hand, excessive beautification and jewellery is not encouraged, because this may impact their masculinity.

In this hadith, the Prophet Muhammad ﷺ explains that wearing gold or silk is prohibited for men. As such, men are not allowed to wear gold in any form, whether watches, rings, or anything else. They are also not allowed to wear real silk, except for a small insignificant amount that was allowed by the Prophet ﷺ in several other ahadith. Exception to wear silk was also given by the Prophet Muhammad ﷺ to some of the Companions who had a skin problem. In this hadith, gold-coloured metals and synthetic silk are not explicitly mentioned. However, it would be preferred to avoid these too, to avoid resembling things which the Prophet ﷺ prohibited and to be protected from the negative assumptions that people may make.

This hadith establishes that gold and silk are two items prohibited for men to wear, but lawful for women to wear. Life on Earth is a test, and this is a fundamental part of Islamic belief. This 'test' does not consist of answering a set of questions, solving problems or writing essays. Test in this life entails avoiding temptations of Satan, abiding by the lawful and abstaining from the unlawful. It is worth noting that the temptation of unlawful items is really what the soul desires. It is important for the believers to avoid and resist this temptation. If one has managed to control themselves and not fall into the soul's base desires, then they have pleased Allah and have passed the test.

In some instances, we have been given a rational explanation as to why an item is unlawful, but in other instances, the reason behind why Allah made something prohibited is not so clear to us. Islam means to submit to Allah and all of His rulings. So, in either case, Muslims are obliged to abstain from whatever Allah prohibits, because we are certain that Allah only commands us to do that which is for our good.

৩৬৩৬

# Greetings of Salām: *Signs of Faith and Love*

عَنْ أَبِى هُرَيْرَةَ قَالَ قَالَ رَسُولُ اللهِ ﷺ وَالَّذِى نَفْسِى بِيَدِهِ
لَاتَدْخُلُوا الْجَنَّةَ حَتَّى تُؤْمِنُوا وَلاَ تُؤْمِنُوا حَتَّى تَحَابُّوا أَوَلاَ أَدُلُّكُمْ
عَلَى شَىْءٍ إِذَا فَعَلْتُمُوهُ تَحَابَبْتُمْ أَفْشُوا السَّلاَمَ بَيْنَكُمْ

Abū Hurayrah ﷺ narrated that the Messenger of Allah ﷺ said: 'By the One in whose Hand is my soul! You will not enter Paradise until you believe, and you will not (truly) believe until you love one another. Shall I not tell you of something which, if you do it, you will love one another? Spread the greetings of *salām* amongst yourselves.'

*A*ssalāmu 'alaykum is the greeting Muslims use to greet each other. It means 'peace be upon you'. The Prophet Muhammad ﷺ taught his followers that greeting one another is from the best of actions and one should greet any Muslim regardless of whether they know each other or not. The Prophet ﷺ also taught Muslims that one of the rights one Muslim has over another is to greet them when meeting them and to respond to their greetings. This simple action plays a great role in bringing the hearts together and in building positive relationships. Establishing a strong bond amongst Muslims is a major objective of Islam. Although it may seem insignificant, it goes a long way in achieving a major part of Islam. There are other examples in the ahadith of actions that seem to look like minor deeds yet carry a lot of weight, such as replying to the person who sneezes, visiting the sick, and the like. Another example of this is the way the Prophet ﷺ consistently reminded the Companions to stand close to one another and keep their rows straight when standing for prayer. He would say, 'Do not differ [when standing in your rows] lest your hearts differ.'[2] This shows that our external attitude can have an impact on our internal attitude. Standing closely next to one another in the rows of the prayer, will lead to our hearts getting closer together and more connected with each other.

The greeting of *salām* is also a special and distinct symbol for Muslims. It is the greetings of Allah and His angels; it is the greeting of the righteous; and it contains many great meanings. When a person greets you with *Assalāmu 'alaykum* they are giving you an indication that you are their brethren in faith, that you are safe and have nothing to fear with respect to them, and that they are there for you if you need anything.

This is the great message *Assalāmu 'alaykum* spreads and consequently it becomes a means for love, respect, care and companionship. This is therefore one of the most basic and important habits a person can have and teach others.

෴

# Offering Sound Advice

عَنْ أَبِي هُرَيْرَةَ أَن رَسُولُ اللَّهِ ﷺ قَالَ الْمُسْتَشَارُ مُؤْتَمَنٌ

Abū Hurayrah ﷺ narrated that the Messenger of Allah
ﷺ said: 'One who is consulted is entrusted.'

Thinking well and speaking well of others is an obligation in
Islam. At the same time, this should not cause us to be naive,
resulting in harm for ourselves or others. Rather, we should be realistic
about people's strengths and weaknesses. The Prophet Muhammad
ﷺ refused to give Abū Dharr ﷺ a leadership position because he
did not view him as capable of taking on such a role. Abū Dharr ﷺ
was a noble Companion with many virtues, but this is not enough
for one to be entrusted with a position which involves taking care of
some of the affairs of people. The same principle should be applied
when someone considers a person for marriage, for a job, as a teacher,
or any other responsibility. This ability to make the right judgement
becomes increasingly important when someone else seeks our advice.

In this hadith, the Prophet Muhammad ﷺ explained that the one who is being consulted is entrusted. This means that they have been entrusted to give the correct information and the most appropriate advice to the best of their ability.

If we are consulted about a relative for marriage, then we must be honest in mentioning his or her strengths and weaknesses. If we conceal the person's weaknesses, then we would be deceiving our brother or sister who is interested in marriage. Similarly, if we are consulted about our views on someone's ability to trade or teach or fulfil a particular job, we should be honest about what we know, provided that we have informed knowledge and are not merely making assumptions. We are not required to bring up someone's past sins, because these should be concealed. However, we must make clear any current weaknesses they have because the person seeking advice trusts us to be honest and may be making a life-changing decision based on our advice. Imam 'Alī ibn al-Madīnī, a leading Hadith scholar, was asked about the strength of his own father as a hadith narrator. Although, he initially hesitated to speak of his father, he made it clear that his father was a weak narrator. His respect for his father did not stop him from speaking the truth and giving sincere advice to the believers, because he was an expert on hadith criticism and was thus entrusted to speak the truth.

# 8

# An Easy Way to Remove Sins

عَنْ عَمْرِو بْنِ عَبَسَةَ قَالَ قَالَ رَسُولُ اللَّهِ ﷺ إِنَّ الْعَبْدَ إِذَا تَوَضَّأَ
فَغَسَلَ يَدَيْهِ خَرَّتْ خَطَايَاهُ مِنْ يَدَيْهِ فَإِذَا غَسَلَ وَجْهَهُ خَرَّتْ
خَطَايَاهُ مِنْ وَجْهِهِ فَإِذَا غَسَلَ ذِرَاعَيْهِ وَمَسَحَ بِرَأْسِهِ خَرَّتْ خَطَايَاهُ
مِنْ ذِرَاعَيْهِ وَرَأْسِهِ فَإِذَا غَسَلَ رِجْلَيْهِ خَرَّتْ خَطَايَاهُ مِنْ رِجْلَيْهِ

‘Amr ibn ‘Abasah ﷺ narrated that the Messenger of Allah
ﷺ said: ‘When a person performs ablution and washes his
hands, his sins exit through his hands. When he washes
his face, his sins exit through his face. When he washes
his forearms and wipes his head, his sins exit through his
forearms and head. When he washes his feet, his sins exit
through his feet.’

It can be easy to think of ablution (*wuḍū'*) as a mere act that we need to do for prayer, and as something mundane. However, the Prophet ﷺ mentioned a number of virtues of *wuḍū'*. *Wuḍū'* is independently a righteous act of worship that we are rewarded for performing in the right manner. When we understand the great virtue of ablution, we put ourselves in the correct frame of mind before prayer. It forms a psychological preparation for the prayer as well as a spiritual purification. The sins that we commit on a daily basis are endless. The eyes alone can cause us to fall into a variety of sins. This includes looking at that which we should be lowering our gazes from, staring at the blessings of others with an envious eye, belittling other people, and seeking out the mistakes of others. The sins of the tongue can be even greater and more common. Backbiting, slandering, lying, swearing, and deceiving are all vices of the tongue that are rampant in most communities. Sometimes we fall into these sins without paying much attention or even realising that we have committed them.

Allah has shown us mercy due to our weakness and opened up so many different doors of seeking forgiveness. Performing *wuḍū'* washes away the sins that we commit using our eyes, mouth, hands and feet. Praying five times a day cleanses us from all minor sins. The Qur'an even teaches us that simply avoiding major sins purifies us from the minor sins. Therefore, when we recognise our desperate need for Allah's forgiveness, we should not make *wuḍū'* except that we view it as a means of purification. This allows us to face Allah in prayer in a pure state. It makes us take our prayers more seriously and lets us experience the great impact of our daily prayers.

෴

# 9

# What to do if a Dog Licks Something

عَنْ أَبِى هُرَيْرَةَ أَنَّ رَسُولَ اللَّهِ ﷺ قَالَ إِذَا شَرِبَ الْكَلْبُ فِى إِنَاءِ
أَحَدِكُمْ فَلْيَغْسِلْهُ سَبْعَ مَرَّاتٍ

Abū Hurayrah ؓ narrated that the Messenger of Allah
ﷺ said: 'If a dog licks the vessel of anyone of you, let him
wash it seven times.'

All animals are a blessing of Allah; they are His creation and a
proof of the majesty of Allah. Humans make use of animals in
different ways, and dogs are very useful animals. Their abilities are
truly amazing. People keep dogs for protection, hunting, helping the
blind, security and many other reasons. Islam has allowed us to keep
dogs for various reasons, including those mentioned above. However,
it should be noted that keeping dogs as pets is not allowed in Islam.
In this hadith, the Prophet Muhammad ﷺ wanted to teach Muslims
what they should do if a dog licked something.

If a dog drinks from a vessel containing water, then the Prophet
ﷺ commanded that the vessel should be washed seven times. Some

narrations also mention adding soil along with the seven washes for additional purification. According to the Hanbali school of thought, using soap or other purifiers can be used instead of soil.

The legal scholars had different understandings of the wisdom behind this Prophetic command. Some of them considered the saliva of dogs to be impure, and hence, in order to use the vessels again in future, they must first be cleansed from the impurity of the dog. Other scholars argue that dogs, along with their saliva, are pure. The requirement to wash therefore is not related to purity, rather it is simply due to the Prophetic command. This is the opinion of Imam Mālik. We may be unaware of the wisdom behind this command because the Prophet ﷺ did not explicitly mention the impurity of the dog. Regardless of their reasoning, scholars agree that washing should take place if a dog drinks from a vessel.

There arises another question: If someone's clothes are licked by a dog or if the dog walks around the house or even the mosque, does it require washing seven times? Most scholars believe dogs are not impure themselves and that it is only their saliva which is considered impure. Therefore, only if their saliva falls in the mosque or house does it require washing. Other scholars believe that the dog itself is impure and therefore the mosque and house need to be washed with water. However, Imam Mālik is of the opinion that washing is not required at all because dogs are pure and the command to wash in the hadith only spoke of washing vessels.

It is interesting to note that dogs used to walk around in the Prophet's mosque and there is no mention of the Prophet ﷺ or the Companions washing the *masjid* because of it. Imam Mālik argues that this proves the purity of dogs and that only those vessels licked by the dog are required to be washed, not other things. According to him, prayer would be valid in clothes that have been licked by a dog. However, it would be better for someone to wash their clothes in order to err on the side of caution.

# 10

# Praying Next to a Menstruating Woman

عَنْ عَائِشَةَ ﷺ قَالَتْ كَانَ رَسُولُ اللَّهِ ﷺ يُصَلِّي وَأَنَا إِلَى جَنْبِهِ وَأَنَا حَائِضٌ وَعَلَيَّ مِرْطٌ لِي وَعَلَيْهِ بَعْضُهُ

'Ā'ishah ﷺ narrated: 'The Messenger of Allah ﷺ
was performing prayer, and I was by his side. I was
menstruating, and I was wearing a wool cloak, and part of
it was over him.'

The monthly menstrual period is a natural biological phenomenon that Allah has decreed for women. Several rulings apply for women during menstruation, such as the impermissibility of prayer, fasting and intimate marital relations. However, besides these rulings, Muslims are taught in the Qur'an and Sunnah that the menstruating woman herself is not physically impure. This means that we are not told to avoid any physical contact with her. Rather, Islam removed these strict teachings that some previous religions, such as Judaism, followed. There are several authentic reports in which 'Ā'ishah ⌖ discusses how the Prophet ⌖ behaved during her menstrual cycle. For example, the Prophet ⌖ would lie on her lap and recite the Qur'an while she was menstruating. He would share the same bed as her and keep her company. We can clearly see from the Sunnah that he would treat his wives normally.

In some religions and some cultures, menstruating women are treated harshly. During their periods, women are expected to stay in an outhouse or a completely different room, and there are restrictions on what they can do. Although Islam rejects all this, it does consider them to be in a state of ritual impurity. Therefore, women do not pray or fast, and they should not stay inside the mosque, according to most scholars.

Intimate details like this were shared by the Prophet's wives because people can easily make incorrect assumptions. They may assume that the prohibition of prayer during menstruation also means that she should keep away from people who are praying and that she should not be touched. A menstruating woman can do the *dhikr* of Allah, read books of knowledge, and attend religious lectures. According to Imam Mālik, she can also recite the Qur'an without touching a copy of the Qur'an. She can thus recite from her mobile phone or another device of that sort. The summary of this discussion is that that this hadith clarifies the nature of interacting with a woman on her cycle, and that there is nothing different or special in this regard except sexual intercourse.

# 11

# *The* Du‘ā’ *after the* Adhān

عَنْ جَابِرِ بْنِ عَبْدِ اللَّهِ قَالَ قَالَ رَسُولُ اللَّهِ ﷺ مَنْ قَالَ حِينَ يَسْمَعُ النِّدَاءَ اللَّهُمَّ رَبَّ هَذِهِ الدَّعْوَةِ التَّامَّةِ وَالصَّلاةِ الْقَائِمَةِ آتِ مُحَمَّدًا الْوَسِيلَةَ وَالْفَضِيلَةَ وَابْعَثْهُ مَقَامًا مَحْمُودًا الَّذِى وَعَدْتَهُ إِلاَّ حَلَّتْ لَهُ الشَّفَاعَةُ يَوْمَ الْقِيَامَةِ

Jābir ibn ‘Abdullāh ﷺ narrated that the Messenger of Allah ﷺ said: ‘Whoever says when he hears the call to the prayer: "O Allah, Lord of this perfect call and the prayer to be offered, grant Muhammad the privilege (of intercession) and also the eminence, and resurrect him to the praised position that You have promised," my intercession for him will be permitted on the Day of Resurrection.'

One of the greatest gifts given to the Prophet Muhammad ﷺ is the right to intercede for his followers. Intercession (*shafā'ah*) refers to someone speaking to a higher authority on our behalf so as to bring us some benefit or protect us from some harm. On the Day of Judgement some people will be allowed to intercede for one another. The Qur'an teaches us that intercession on this great day is only for those whom Allah has given permission to intercede, and intercession will only be accepted for those whom Allah is pleased with. The greatest verse in the Qur'an, *Āyat al-Kursī*, mentions, *'Who could possibly intercede with Him [Allah] without His permission?'* (*al-Baqarah* 2: 255)

The Qur'an also explains that intercession is not granted for anyone. One must do good deeds and have faith in their heart for any intercession to be accepted on their behalf. Allah says, *'And they [righteous servants] do not intercede except for those whom He is pleased with'* (*al-Anbiyā'* 21: 28). In another hadith, Abū Hurayrah ﷺ asked the Prophet Muhammad ﷺ about the person most deserving of his intercession. The Prophet ﷺ replied, 'The one who says *"Lā ilāha illa Allāh"* (There is no god except Allah) sincerely from his heart.'

From the people allowed to intercede are the Prophets of Allah, friends and family. The Prophet ﷺ told us that when people enter Jannah, some of them will realise that their friends are not with them, so they will say: 'O Allah, our brothers; they used to pray and fast with us.' Allah Almighty will say, 'Go and take out anyone who you find with a corn's worth of faith.' However, the greatest intercession will be that of the Prophet Muhammad ﷺ, because nobody is more beloved to Allah than this Prophet. He will intercede for the sinners from his followers who are doomed to the punishment of Hell and also for the righteous believers for their rank to be raised. Those who love him more than their own selves and follow his Sunnah will be most worthy of his intercession.

In this hadith, the Prophet ﷺ directs Muslims towards a simple action to gain his intercession before Allah, Most High. This action is an opportunity that presents itself many times a day. It is an easy way of ensuring the Prophet's intercession. All we have to do is listen to the *adhān* and then recite this supplication:

*Allāhumma Rabba hādhihid-daʿwatit-tāmmah waṣ-ṣalātil-qāʾimah, āti Muḥammadanil-waṣīlata wal-faḍīlah, wabʿathhu maqāman maḥmūdan-illadhī waʿadtah*

*O Allah, Lord of this perfect call and the prayer to be offered, grant Muhammad the privilege (of intercession) and also the eminence, and resurrect him to the praised position that You have promised.*

What a missed opportunity it would be for someone to not be included in receiving intercession from the Prophet Muhammad ﷺ because they failed to recite this simple *duʿāʾ* after the *adhān*.

༺☙༻

# 12

# The Comparison of this World to the Hereafter

عَنْ قَيْسِ بْنِ أَبِى حَازِمٍ قَالَ سَمِعْتُ الْمُسْتَوْرِدَ أَخَا بَنِى فِهْرٍ يَقُولُ سَمِعْتُ رَسُولَ اللَّهِ ﷺ يَقُولُ مَا مَثَلُ الدُّنْيَا فِى الْآخِرَةِ إِلاَّ مَثَلُ مَا يَجْعَلُ أَحَدُكُمْ إِصْبَعَهُ فِى الْيَمِّ فَلْيَنْظُرْ بِمَ يَرْجِعُ

Mustawrid, a brother of [the tribe of] Banū Fihr, said:
'I heard the Messenger of Allah ﷺ say: "The likeness of this world in comparison to the Hereafter is that of one of you dipping his finger into the sea; let him see what he brings back."'

The Qur'an constantly reminds us of the stark difference between this life and the Hereafter, making it clear that this life is insignificant in comparison to the next one. For example, Allah says in the Qur'an: *'This worldly life is no more than play and amusement, but far better is the [eternal] home of the Hereafter for those mindful [of Allah].*

*Will you not then understand?'* (*al-Anʿām* 6: 32) Allah Almighty also says: *'Allah expands the provision for whom He wills and narrows it (for whom He wills). They are happy with the worldly life, while the worldly life, compared to the Hereafter, is nothing but a little enjoyment'* (*al-Raʿd* 13: 26).

The comparison between the two lives is sometimes made through similes that reinforce this fact into our minds and hearts. In this hadith, the Prophet ﷺ gives us an example of the reality of this life. If someone dipped their finger into the sea and took it out, how much water would they have on their finger compared to what still remains in the sea? It is almost nothing. This amount is what this life is worth when we compare it to the everlasting life that awaits us.

When Allah strikes an example in the Qur'an or through his Prophet ﷺ, it is not intended to be an exaggeration. Rather, Allah is the most truthful in speech and His descriptions are the most accurate. When we understand and have full conviction of the reality of this life, we are more able to put our thoughts, actions and lifestyle into perspective.

This hadith wants to teach Muslims to not give priority to this life, but to give priority to the life after this. What Muslims can expect from life in this world in comparison to the Hereafter is like a drop of water in an ocean. This is mind-blowing. Therefore, sacrificing for the sake of Allah and being obedient to Him is the only reasonable thing to do. In this context, the worship of other than Allah, following sinful desires, oppressing others, and other acts of transgression and misguidance will be a cause of great regret in the afterlife, because we will then truly understand that those things were not worth it. The one who realises the true status of this life would never ruin their afterlife for the sake of the short-lived false hopes of this life.

# 13

# The Reward of the Muezzin

عَنْ أَبِي هُرَيْرَةَ قَالَ سَمِعْتُ مِنْ فِي رَسُولِ اللَّهِ ﷺ يَقُولُ الْمُؤَذِّنُ يُغْفَرُ لَهُ مَدَّ صَوْتِهِ وَيَسْتَغْفِرُ لَهُ كُلُّ رَطْبٍ وَيَابِسٍ وَشَاهِدُ الصَّلاَةِ يُكْتَبُ لَهُ خَمْسٌ وَعِشْرُونَ حَسَنَةً وَيُكَفَّرُ عَنْهُ مَا بَيْنَهُمَا

Abū Hurayrah ﷺ said: 'I heard from the mouth of the Messenger of Allah ﷺ: "The sins of the caller to prayer (muezzin) will be forgiven as far as his voice reaches, and every wet and dry thing will pray for his forgiveness. For the one who attends the prayer, twenty-five good deeds will be recorded, and it is an expiation (for sins committed) between them (two prayers)."'

Most Muslims understand how to pray and what should be done before and after the prayer. However, most are not aware of the great rewards and virtues that come with the prayer itself and all those other acts of worship that are connected to the prayer. There is great reward in the acts of *wuḍū'*, walking to the prayer, waiting for the prayer, performing the *adhān* (call to prayer), remembering Allah after the prayer, and walking back from the prayer. If we are conscious of these realities, our prayers would be much more focused and it would have a greater impact on our lives. In this hadith, the Prophet Muhammad ﷺ teaches us that attending the prayer in congregation is twenty-five times better than praying individually. The hadith also mentions that obligatory prayers result in the purification from all minor sins that may have occurred between a prayer and the one before it.

Another important Sunnah discussed in the hadith is the call to prayer (*adhān*). Making the call to prayer is a means of forgiveness. Not only that, but every object around the caller to prayer makes supplication for that person's forgiveness. Although we cannot comprehend how lifeless objects seek forgiveness for people, the One who created them told us that this happens, so we know that it is true. One of the main objectives of the *adhān* is to call people to pray and to make them aware of its time. However, the *adhān* itself is a Sunnah which should be done even when there are only few people present. The Prophet ﷺ told two people who wanted to travel that when the time of prayer comes, they should make the *adhān* and *iqāmah*, and the older of the two should lead the prayer. The great Companion, Abū Saʿīd al-Khudrī ﷺ, even advised a person who prays alone in his farm to raise his voice when calling the *adhān* at the time of prayer. He told him that he heard the Prophet ﷺ saying that any *jinn*, human or anything for that matter that hears his *adhān* will be a witness for him on the Day of Judgement.

# 14

# Building a Mosque for the Sake of Allah

عَنْ جَابِرِ بْنِ عَبْدِ اللَّهِ أَنَّ رَسُولَ اللَّهِ ﷺ قَالَ مَنْ بَنَى مَسْجِدًا
لِلَّهِ كَمَفْحَصِ قَطَاةٍ أَوْ أَصْغَرَ بَنَى اللَّهُ لَهُ بَيْتًا فِي الْجَنَّةِ

Jābir ibn 'Abdullāh ؓ narrated that the Messenger of
Allah ﷺ said: 'Whoever builds a mosque for the sake of
Allah, like a sparrow's nest or even smaller, Allah will
build for him a house in Paradise.'

Good deeds are of two types. The first are personal acts of worship
that Muslims perform as acts of individual devotion to Allah.
This includes things such as prayer, remembering Allah, hajj, 'umrah,
and making du'ā'. The second type is that which has a wider impact
on others. This includes acts such as imparting knowledge, writing
books, giving in charity, building mosques and schools, and other
similar actions. Both types of deeds are essential for individuals and
societies. However, the second type is often of superior reward, second

to obligations. This is because individual acts of voluntary worship are mostly of benefit only for the individual performing them. On the other hand, the second type of good deeds mentioned above extends to others and maximises the amount of good that stems from them. It is because of this very principle that public sin is considered far worse than private sin in Islam, as the former can encourage others to sin and results in the normalisation of immorality. Similarly, doing something which others continue to benefit from is of great reward, because it encourages the spread of goodness.

The Prophet Muhammad ﷺ said: 'Whoever introduces a good practice that is followed after him, will have a reward for that and the equivalent of their reward, without that detracting from their reward in the slightest. [Similarly] whoever introduces an evil practice that is followed after him, will bear the burden of sin for that and the equivalent of their burden of sin, without that detracting from their burden in the slightest.'[3] Of course, no mosque can be the size of a sparrow's nest, but in this hadith, the Prophet ﷺ is emphasising the great virtue of helping build a mosque, even if it is through just a small contribution. The mosques are the houses of Allah, places of worship, places of learning, and hubs for bringing the community together. They play an essential role in society. Having said this, we must ensure that we are not simply building mosques just for the sake of it; instead, we should check to see that they are fulfilling their tasks within the society to the highest level possible.

<hr />

3    Ibn Majah, *Sunan Ibn Majah*, Hadith no. 207

# History of the
# Prophet's Mosque

عَنْ أَنَسِ بْنِ مَالِكٍ قَالَ كَانَ مَوْضِعُ مَسْجِدِ النَّبِيِّ ﷺ لِبَنِى
النَّجَّارِ وَكَانَ فِيهِ نَخْلٌ وَمَقَابِرُ لِلْمُشْرِكِينَ فَقَالَ لَهُمُ النَّبِيُّ ﷺ
ثَامِنُونِي بِهِ قَالُوا لاَ نَأْخُذُ لَهُ ثَمَنًا أَبَدًا قَالَ فَكَانَ النَّبِيُّ ﷺ يَبْنِيهِ
وَهُمْ يُنَاوِلُونَهُ وَالنَّبِيُّ ﷺ يَقُولُ أَلاَ إِنَّ الْعَيْشَ عَيْشُ الآخِرَةِ فَاغْفِرْ
لِلأَنْصَارِ وَالْمُهَاجِرَةِ قَالَ وَكَانَ النَّبِيُّ ﷺ يُصَلِّى قَبْلَ أَنْ يَبْنِىَ
الْمَسْجِدَ حَيْثُ أَدْرَكَتْهُ الصَّلاَةُ

Anas ibn Malik ﷺ said: 'The location where the Prophet's mosque was built belonged to Banū al-Najjār. In it there were date-palm trees and graves of the idolaters. The Prophet ﷺ said to them: "Name its price." They said: "We will never take any money for it." The Prophet ﷺ built it and they were assisting him, and the Prophet ﷺ was

saying: "The real life is the life of the Hereafter so forgive
the Anṣār and the Muhājirūn." Before the mosque was
built, the Prophet ﷺ would perform prayer wherever he
was when the time for prayer came.'

When the Prophet Muhammad ﷺ arrived in Madinah, one of
the first things that he did was to establish the mosque, *Masjid
al-Nabawī*. This mosque became the point of congregation for the
Muslims, a centre for learning, and a place of refuge for those who
needed it. The Prophet's mosque became a central part of the Muslim
community newly established in Madinah. It would be the first point
of contact for people who wanted to learn about Islam. The regular
prayers at the mosque prayed in congregation strengthened the bond
that already existed between the Muslims.

Many things could be said about the vital role played by a mosque
in establishing, stabilising, and developing the community. At a
time in which methods of preaching and imparting knowledge are
so varied, it becomes all the more important to study the role the
Prophet's mosque played in the early Muslim community. This way,
Muslims today have a Prophetic model which acts as an essential
starting point for developing their communities.

The Prophet Muhammad ﷺ placed most of his initial efforts
into teaching about Allah, the afterlife, and purifying the hearts.
This came before the detailed legal obligations which were mainly
introduced in Madinah after thirteen or more years of Prophethood.
This spiritual development that was built into the Muslims by the
Prophet ﷺ made them prepared to give and sacrifice for the sake
of Allah. The Muslims who migrated from Makkah to Madinah
(known as the Muhājirūn) were paired with their brothers from the
Anṣār who were the residents of Madinah. The Anṣār were willing

to share their homes, their wealth, and everything they owned with their brothers from the Muhājirūn. This attitude of sacrifice and their willingness to give is what made the first Muslim generation so great. We see an excellent example of this in those from the tribe of Banū al-Najjār who refused to take any money for their land on which the Prophet 🕌 wanted to build a mosque.

# 16

# *How to Pray*

عَنْ مُحَمَّدُ بْنُ عَمْرِو بْنِ عَطَاءٍ عَنْ أَبِي حُمَيْدٍ السَّاعِدِيّ قَالَ
سَمِعْتُهُ وَهُوَ فِي عَشَرَةٍ مِنْ أَصْحَابِ رَسُولِ اللهِ ﷺ أَحَدُهُمْ أَبُو
قَتَادَةَ بْنُ رِبْعِيّ قَالَ أَنَا أَعْلَمُكُمْ بِصَلَاةِ رَسُولِ اللهِ ﷺ كَانَ إِذَا
قَامَ فِي الصَّلَاةِ اعْتَدَلَ قَائِمًا وَرَفَعَ يَدَيْهِ حَتَّى يُحَاذِيَ بِهِمَا مَنْكِبَيْهِ
ثُمَّ قَالَ اللهُ أَكْبَرُ وَإِذَا أَرَادَ أَنْ يَرْكَعَ رَفَعَ يَدَيْهِ حَتَّى يُحَاذِيَ بِهِمَا
مَنْكِبَيْهِ فَإِذَا قَالَ سَمِعَ اللهُ لِمَنْ حَمِدَهُ رَفَعَ يَدَيْهِ فَاعْتَدَلَ فَإِذَا قَامَ
مِنَ الثِّنْتَيْنِ كَبَّرَ وَرَفَعَ يَدَيْهِ حَتَّى يُحَاذِيَ بِهِمَا مَنْكِبَيْهِ كَمَا صَنَعَ
حِينَ افْتَتَحَ الصَّلَاةَ

Muḥammad ibn 'Amr ibn 'Aṭā' said, concerning Abū
Ḥumayd Al-Sā'idī: 'I heard him when he was among ten
of the Companions of the Messenger of Allah ﷺ, one of

whom was Abū Qatādah ibn Rib'ī, saying: "I am the most knowledgeable of you about the prayer of the Messenger of Allah ﷺ. When he stood up for prayer, he stood up straight and raised his hands until they were parallel to his shoulders, then he said: 'Allāhu Akbar' (Allah is the Greatest). When he wanted to bow, he raised his hands until they were parallel to his shoulders. When he said 'Sami' Allāhu liman ḥamidah' (Allah hears those who praise Him), he raised his hands and stood up straight.

When he stood up after two rak'ahs, he said 'Allāhu Akbar' and raised his hands until they were parallel to his shoulders, as he did when he started the prayer.'"

Allah created mankind to worship Him alone and to reject worshipping anything else. This is the greatest purpose of our creation. However, we have not been left to ourselves to worship as we see fit. The Prophet Muhammad ﷺ was sent by Allah Almighty to teach people how to worship Allah correctly. Without the Prophet ﷺ, every person may decide how to go about glorifying and worshipping Allah on their own, which would certainly lead to errors and ignorant practices. Some people would abstain from any worship and instead suffice with the claim that they love Allah in their hearts; while others would go to extremes that may even lead to harming others, justifying this with the claim that it is done for Allah. In relation to the greatest act of worship in Islam, the Prophet Muhammad ﷺ said, 'Pray as you have seen me pray.'[4] Just as it is important to pray sincerely to Allah

---

4    Al-Bukhari, *Sahih al-Bukhari*, Hadith no. 327

with total concentration, it is necessary to pray exactly as the Prophet ﷺ taught us.

There are many reports from the Companions explaining how the Prophet ﷺ prayed. This hadith is particularly important in this regard, because it was mentioned by Abū Ḥumayd in the presence of a number of other Companions who approved his explanation of the Prophet's prayer. This narration mentions the four places at which the Prophet ﷺ used to raise his hands until they were roughly at the same level as his shoulders. These places are at the beginning of the prayer, just before bowing (*rukūʿ*), when standing up from bowing, and when standing up from the second unit (*rakʿah*). Most of the narrations that describe the Prophet's prayer mention raising the hands at only the first three places, so these are additionally recommended and considered a Sunnah by most of the scholars. The fourth place is also mentioned authentically by some Companions, like in this hadith here, and thus it would be recommended to sometimes do this also.

# 17

# Prostration to Allah

عَنْ أَبِي هُرَيْرَةَ قَالَ قَالَ رَسُولُ اللَّهِ ﷺ إِذَا قَرَأَ ابْنُ آدَمَ السَّجْدَةَ فَسَجَدَ اعْتَزَلَ الشَّيْطَانُ يَبْكِي يَقُولُ يَا وَيْلَهُ أُمِرَ ابْنُ آدَمَ بِالسُّجُودِ فَسَجَدَ فَلَهُ الْجَنَّةُ وَأُمِرْتُ بِالسُّجُودِ فَأَبَيْتُ فَلِيَ النَّارُ

Abū Hurayrah ﷺ narrated that the Messenger of Allah ﷺ said: 'When a son of Adam recites a *sajdah* (verse of prostration) and prostrates, Satan withdraws weeping, saying: "Woe to me! The son of Adam was commanded to prostrate, and he prostrated, and Paradise will be his; and I was commanded to prostrate, and I refused, so I am doomed to Hell."'

It is important to consider the meanings behind the physical aspects of acts of worship. This is particularly important in relation to prayer, because its repetitive nature on a daily basis can make it easy to lose sight of its value. Prostration (*sujūd*) especially has a distinct significance, because it summarises the nature of the relationship between a servant and their Lord. When a person places their head on the ground, they are showing a willingness to be humble, an understanding of their need, and an admittance of their weakness. It is this humility which raises a person in the Sight of Allah. The Prophet Muhammad ﷺ said: 'Whoever humbles himself for Allah, Allah will raise his status.'[5] Our natural human pride and self-respect prevents us from lowering our heads for anyone, except for those whom we have utmost respect towards. Since nobody other than Allah is worthy of being shown such respect and humility, Islam has made it forbidden for a Muslim to prostrate to anyone besides Allah.

Satan understood the meaning of humility implied by prostration; hence arrogance prevented him from obeying Allah's command to prostrate. He felt more superior than to prostrate to someone created by Allah, although this was a direct command by Allah for him to do it. Satan's arrogance led to humiliation in this life, while a greater humiliation awaits him and his followers in the afterlife. A person is closest to Allah when they are in a state of prostration. It is a time in which our supplications are more likely to be accepted as the Prophet ﷺ told us. These are meanings which we should bear in mind each time we fall into prostration, whether this is while reciting verses of the Qur'an or during our regular prayers. Perhaps doing so will lead to Allah honouring us and raising our status in this life and the next.

༺ஐ༻

---

5    Muslim, *Sahih Muslim*, Hadith no. 2588

# The Virtue of Twelve Units of Voluntary Prayers

عَنْ عَائِشَةَ قَالَتْ قَالَ رَسُولُ اللهِ ﷺ مَنْ ثَابَرَ عَلَى ثِنْتَىْ عَشْرَةَ
رَكْعَةً مِنَ السُّنَّةِ بُنِيَ لَهُ بَيْتٌ فِي الْجَنَّةِ أَرْبَع قَبْلَ الظُّهْرِ وَرَكْعَتَيْنِ
بَعْدَ الظُّهْرِ وَرَكْعَتَيْنِ بَعْدَ الْمَغْرِبِ وَرَكْعَتَيْنِ بَعْدَ الْعِشَاءِ وَرَكْعَتَيْنِ
قَبْلَ الْفَجْرِ

'Ā'ishah ◈ narrated that the Messenger of Allah ﷺ
said: 'Whoever persists in performing twelve units
(*rak'ah*) from the Sunnah, a house will be built for him
in Paradise: four before Ẓuhr, two units after Ẓuhr, two
units after Maghrib, two units after 'Ishā' and two units
before Fajr.'

Voluntary acts of worship makes us draw closer to Allah. We
should be mindful that the more we fill our time with noble
voluntary acts, the less likely we are to neglect obligatory acts of

worship. Similarly, the more we keep away from things which are disliked, the less likely it is for us to fall into sin. After belief in Allah and His Messenger, the five daily prayers are the greatest of the pillars of Islam. Voluntary prayers are also of great virtue because they act as a protection for other obligatory acts of worship. This means that on the Day of Judgement, our voluntary prayers will make up for any deficiencies found in our obligatory prayers. The Prophet Muhammad ﷺ said: 'The first thing for which a person will be brought to account on the Day of Resurrection will be his *ṣalāh*. If it is found to be complete then it will be recorded as complete, and if anything is lacking, Allah will say to the angels: "Look and see if you can find any voluntary prayers with which to complete what he neglected of his obligatory prayers." Then the rest of his deeds will be reckoned in like manner.'[6]

These voluntary prayers which the Prophet ﷺ would regularly perform would be done by him at home. He said: 'The best prayer is that done at home, except for the [five] obligatory prayers.'[7] Praying at home helps with not only maintaining sincerity but also in ensuring that our homes are not being left for purely worldly matters, but that they contain the remembrance of Allah too. However, if it is likely that one would forget or miss the voluntary prayers by trying to pray at home, then they should pray them at the mosque, however, one should try to make voluntary prayer at home a habit.

The twelve units mentioned in the hadith are not all of equal emphasis in the Sunnah. The Prophet ﷺ would at times miss some of them when travelling. However, he gave extra attention to the two units before the Fajr prayer. One can thus start by regularly praying these two units until they slowly make a habit of praying all twelve units.

---

6   Ibn Majah, *Sunan Ibn Majah*, Hadith no. 1426

7   Al-Bukhari, *Sahih al-Bukhari*, Hadith no. 6113

# *The* Witr *Prayer*

عَنْ أُبَيِّ بنِ كَعْبٍ قَالَ كَانَ رَسُولُ اللّٰه ﷺ يُوتِرُ بِـ سَبِّح اسْمَ رَبِّكَ الأَعْلَى   وَ   قُلْ يَا أَيُّهَا الْكَافِرُونَ   وَ   قُلْ هُوَ اللّٰهُ أَحَدٌ

Ubayy ibn Ka'b ﷺ said: 'The Messenger of Allah ﷺ used to perform *witr* and recite: "Glorify the Name of your Lord the Most High,"[8] "Say: O you disbelievers!"[9] and "Say: Allah is One."'[10]

The five daily prayers are the only regular daily prayers which are compulsory. However, the Prophet Muhammad ﷺ informed his followers of another important prayer which is the *witr* prayer. This is a very important prayer, and most scholars believe it to be a strongly

---

8  Surah al-A'la (87)

9  Surah al-Kafirun (109)

10  Surah al-Ikhlas (112)

recommended Sunnah, but Imam Abū Ḥanīfah regarded it as *wājib* (obligatory).

The *witr* prayer was performed by the Prophet Muhammad ﷺ consistently every night between the 'Ishā' and Fajr prayer without fail. The Prophet's wife 'Ā'ishah ﷺ recalls the time the Prophet ﷺ would pray *witr*; she said at times the Prophet prayed the *witr* prayer at the beginning of the night, and at times in the middle, and at times towards the end of the night shortly before Fajr (dawn). However, eventually he would pray it mostly in the final third of the night after completing the night prayer (*qiyām al-layl*). This is an especially virtuous time to pray, supplicate, and seek forgiveness. The Prophet ﷺ said: 'Allah descends in the final third of every night and says, is there anyone seeking forgiveness so that I can forgive them, is there anyone supplicating so that I may give them.'

The *witr* prayer is ideally prayed as three units (*rak'ah*s), although many scholars allow it to be prayed as just one unit, such as Imam Shāfi'ī and Imam Aḥmad ibn Ḥanbal. Some of the Companions would pray *witr* as only one unit. In another hadith, the Prophet ﷺ said that the *witr* prayer should be the last prayer that one prays in the night.[11] Hence, if someone is staying up all night or they normally wake up during the final third of the night, they should delay the *witr* prayer. However, the Prophet ﷺ encouraged some Companions to pray *witr* before they go to sleep. This should be done by those who do not think they will wake up towards the end of the night before Fajr. If someone prayed *witr* straight after 'Ishā' and then found themselves awake before Fajr, they can still perform as many units of voluntary prayer as they like, but they should not repeat the *witr* prayer because *witr* is prayed only once a night.

This hadith teaches Muslims what the Prophet Muhammad ﷺ used to recite during the *witr* prayer. Although it is not obligatory

---

11   Al-Bukhari, *Sahih al-Bukhari*, Hadith no. 472

to recite what he recited, it is however, deeply rewardable to do so regularly. It is our duty, as Muslims to follow the Prophet Muhammad ﷺ as much as we can, and this is an easy Sunnah we can practise in our lives.

৩৩৩

# The Reward of Fasting

عَنْ أَبِي هُرَيْرَةَ قَالَ قَالَ رَسُولُ اللَّهِ ﷺ كُلُّ عَمَلِ ابْنِ آدَمَ يُضَاعَفُ
الْحَسَنَةُ بِعَشْرِ أَمْثَالِهَا إِلَى سَبْعِمِائَةِ ضِعْفٍ إِلَى مَا شَاءَ اللَّهُ يَقُولُ
اللَّهُ إِلاَّ الصَّوْمَ فَإِنَّهُ لِي وَأَنَا أَجْزِي بِهِ يَدَعُ شَهْوَتَهُ وَطَعَامَهُ مِنْ أَجْلِي
لِلصَّائِمِ فَرْحَتَانِ فَرْحَةٌ عِنْدَ فِطْرِهِ وَفَرْحَةٌ عِنْدَ لِقَاءِ رَبِّهِ وَلَخُلُوفُ
فَمِ الصَّائِمِ أَطْيَبُ عِنْدَ اللَّهِ مِنْ رِيحِ الْمِسْكِ

Abū Hurayrah ◈ narrated that the Messenger of Allah
◈ said: 'Every good deed of the son of Adam will be
multiplied manifold. A good deed will be multiplied ten
times up to as many as seven hundred times, or as much
as Allah wills. Allah says: "Except for fasting, which is
for Me and I shall reward for it. He [the fasting person]
gives up his desire and his food for My sake." The fasting

person has two joys: one when he breaks his fast and another when he meets his Lord. The smell that comes from the mouth of a fasting person is better before Allah than the fragrance of musk.'

The vast mercy of Allah upon us means that we will be admitted into Paradise provided our deeds are done with sincere effort, even if they are few. This hadith mentions a principle that is established in the Qur'an where Allah Almighty says: 'Whoever comes with a good deed will be rewarded tenfold' (al-An'ām 6: 160). In another verse, Allah Almighty states: 'The example of those who spend their wealth in the cause of Allah is that of a grain that sprouts into seven ears, each bearing one hundred grains. And Allah multiplies [the reward even more] to whoever He wills' (al-Baqarah 2: 261).

Every good deed done with sincerity is multiplied in its rewards, but the Prophet ﷺ told us that a sin committed is not multiplied in its recompense. This means that one would have to commit so many more sins than virtuous deeds for their sins to outweigh their good deeds. This is a mercy Allah has bestowed upon us, because He is the Most Merciful and because He is aware of our weakness. Allah says: 'Allah intends to make things easy on you. And man has been created weak' (al-Nisā' 4: 28). Knowing this fact, we must never allow a sin that we commit make us lose our morale. Instead, we should immediately do as much good as we can to replace the sin just committed.

This hadith teaches Muslims an important theological point of how Allah rewards people for doing good deeds. For example, when a person prays or gives money to charity, how much reward do they receive? The Prophet ﷺ told us that Allah grants multiples of a person's reward (thawāb or spiritual credit); it can be multiplied ten times and up to as many as seven hundred times, or as much as Allah wills, depending on how the act of worship was done and the level of sincerity involved. Hence, there is a reward scale and it is capped at a certain level. This, however, does not apply to fasting. Fasting is such a special act of worship to Allah that He has taken it off the scale and He will give the person fasting limitless reward as much as He sees fit.

Fasting has a special status, and thus the hadith tells us that its reward is taken care of by Allah without account. This is because fasting involves disciplining the self from worldly matters which are otherwise permissible and giving up desires that are beloved to humans. The Prophet Muhammad ﷺ then told us that the fasting person finds joy when they complete the fast, but even greater joy when they meet their Lord. This is when we will see the fruits of our efforts and enjoy the rewards for the patience we exercised when fasting.

# 21

# *Fasting Three Days a Month*

عَنْ عَائِشَةَ أَنَّهَا قَالَتْ كَانَ رَسُولُ اللَّهِ ﷺ يَصُومُ ثَلاَثَةَ أَيَّامٍ مِنْ كُلِّ شَهْرٍ قُلْتُ مِنْ أَيِّهِ قَالَتْ لَمْ يَكُنْ يُبَالِي مِنْ أَيِّهِ كَانَ

It is narrated that 'Ā'ishah ﷺ said: 'The Messenger of Allah ﷺ used to fast three days of each month.' I said: 'Which were they?' She said: 'He did not care which days they were.'

The Prophet Muhammad ﷺ taught his followers that voluntary acts of worship are best when they are consistent even if they are little. Fasting outside of Ramadan is a voluntary act of worship that has many benefits spiritually and physically. There are a number of ahadith which encourage fasting on the day of Ashura, the 9th of Dhū al-Ḥijjah, on Mondays and Thursdays, and other times. For example, Abū Qatādah al-Anṣārī ﷺ narrates that the Messenger of Allah ﷺ was asked about fasting on Mondays. He said: 'On that day I was born, and on it the Revelation came to me.'[12] Abū Hurayrah ﷺ also narrates the Messenger of Allah ﷺ said: 'Deeds are raised to Allah on Mondays and Thursdays, and I like my deeds to be raised when I am fasting.'[13]

Fasting on three days of each month has also been mentioned in many ahadith. For example, it was narrated that Abū Hurayrah ﷺ said: 'My beloved friend (i.e., the Prophet ﷺ) advised me to do three things which I will not give up until I die: fasting three days of each month, praying mid-morning (*ḍuḥā*), and praying *witr* before sleeping.'

The aim of the hadith was to point out that the Prophet ﷺ fasted consistently every month. If a person is able to fast every Monday and Thursday, then that is better, because it means that a person will fast eight days a month. This may not be possible for many people, and so the Prophet ﷺ encouraged fasting at least three days a month.

Other ahadith suggest that the Prophet Muhammad ﷺ encouraged Muslims to fast during the *Ayyām al-Bīḍ*. These days are when the moon is full, namely the 13th, 14th and 15th of each lunar month. However, this may also not be possible for some but in this hadith of Abū Hurayrah ﷺ, the Prophet Muhammad ﷺ encouraged fasting any three days of every month. This gives us the opportunity to fast any days which are convenient for us. The three days of each month may be fasted at the beginning of the month, in the middle or at the end, and may be done separately or consecutively.

The message we get from all the ahadith narrated regarding voluntary fasting is that it is best to fast regularly, but not daily. Consistency is more important than large amounts of inconsistent worship. Hence, the Prophet ﷺ advised a number of Companions to fast three days a month, because this is an action that can easily be maintained consistently with only a bit of practice.

---

12 Muslim, *Sahih Muslim*, Hadith no. 1162

13 Nasa'i, *Sunan al-Nasa'i*, Hadith no. 2358

# 22

# Gentleness

عَنْ أَبِى هُرَيْرَةَ عَنِ النَّبِيِّ ﷺ قَالَ إِنَّ اللَّهَ رَفِيقٌ يُحِبُّ الرِّفْقَ
وَيُعْطِى عَلَيْهِ مَا لاَ يُعْطِى عَلَى الْعُنْفِ

It was narrated from Abū Hurayrah ﷺ that the Messenger
of Allah ﷺ said: 'Allah is Gentle and loves gentleness, and
He grants reward for it that which He does not grant for
harshness.'

Gentleness is a mark of nobility. Everyone expects to be treated
with gentleness and appreciates when they have been treated
in such a way. The Qur'an talks about gentleness and kindness on
many occasions, and it encourages believers to adopt a behaviour that
promotes gentleness.

Every person must show gentleness to those around them. It is a
fact that people will get in the way of others and cause them annoyance.
It is at that moment that gentleness should be adopted rather than

harshness. Parents must be gentle with their children when they are misbehaving. If they accidently break something, disciplining them harshly may not be the best thing to do.

When parents teach their children gentleness, they will learn to be gentle towards everyone around them, including the parents themselves when they grow old. Islam dictates that children must be gentle towards parents, especially elderly parents. It is very natural that due to old age, our parents become annoying and cause us inconvenience, but we must remember that as children we caused the same inconvenience to them yet they did not turn their backs on us.

Teachers need to be gentle towards their students and when they deserve punishment it should be fair and compassionate. Older siblings must be gentle to towards their younger siblings. Husband and wife must show gentleness towards each other, and anyone in authority must show gentleness towards those under their responsibility.

This hadith teaches us a simple message. It is a message that Allah is gentle, and He loves gentleness. So, if a person wants to get closer to Allah, they must be gentle towards others. If a person shows gentleness towards others, then Allah will reward them and if they fail to do so, they lose an opportunity to earn reward as harshness gains no reward from Allah.. The Prophet ﷺ would even encourage being gentle with his enemies. In one incident, the Prophet ﷺ was greeted by some Jews, who instead of saying, '*Assalāmu 'alaykum*', said, '*Assāmu 'alaykum*', which means, 'May death be upon you.' The Prophet's wife, 'Ā'ishah ﵂, became very upset and began insulting them. However, the Prophet ﷺ did not want her doing that and told her to be gentle with her words.

Being gentle does not cost money. It is about training yourself to express it and to behave towards others in a gentle manner. Using kind words of comfort, showing empathy and sympathy are all traits of gentleness.

# The Prohibited Days to Fast

عَنْ أَبِي عُبَيْدٍ قَالَ شَهِدْتُ الْعِيدَ مَعَ عُمَرَ بْنِ الْخَطَّابِ فَبَدَأَ
بِالصَّلاَةِ قَبْلَ الْخُطْبَةِ فَقَالَ إِنَّ رَسُولَ اللَّهِ ﷺ نَهَى عَنْ صِيَام
هَذَيْنِ الْيَوْمَيْنِ يَوْمُ الْفِطْرِ وَيَوْمُ الأَضْحَى أَمَّا يَوْمُ الْفِطْرِ فَيَوْمُ
فِطْرِكُمْ مِنْ صِيَامِكُمْ وَيَوْمُ الأَضْحَى تَأْكُلُونَ فِيهِ مِنْ لَحْمِ
نُسُكِكُمْ

It was narrated that Abū 'Ubayd said: 'I was present for Eid with Umar ibn al-Khaṭṭāb. He started with the prayer before the sermon and said: "The Messenger of Allah ﷺ forbade fasting on these two days: the Day of Fitr and the Day of Adha. As for the Day of Fitr, it is the day when you break your fast, and on the Day of Adha you eat the meat of your sacrifices."'

This hadith teaches three important lessons. Firstly, the special prayers performed on the Eid day consist of two units of prayer. After that there are two short sermons. Unlike the Friday prayer, the sermons are after the prayer and not before it. The second important lesson is that the Prophet Muhammad ﷺ prohibited observing fasts on the Eid days. There is a time and place for everything in Islam. Every nation, community and religion has days where they would celebrate an event and have fun. On that day there should be no work if it can be avoided. It is important to have such days in order to take a break from the serious nature of the world. It is an opportunity for families and friends to get together and share food with one another. Hence, it is self-defeating if a person fasts on a day they are supposed to be celebrating.

The third and final lesson we can learn from this hadith is that Islam is a rational religion and its laws are logical. Sometimes the reasons as to why certain things are forbidden are mentioned and at other times they are not. In the second case, scholars can deduce the logic behind the prohibition using their reasoning (*ijtihād*). The reason fasting on the festival of Eid al-Fitr is prohibited is because it marks the end of an entire month of fasting. This is an achievement and everyone needs to celebrate this moment. It also makes the fasting of the month of Ramadan a clearly distinct act of worship—the very reason for which the Prophet ﷺ discouraged us from fasting a day or two before Ramadan and prohibited us from fasting the day after Ramadan, which is the day of Eid. In like manner, Eid al-Adha is when the sacrifice is made and there is plenty of meat available. It makes little sense to fast when this meat should be cooked and enjoyed. These two days should be marked with food, drink and plenty of merriment. It is for this reason that Islam has prohibited anyone from fasting on these days.

# *Feeding a Fasting Person*

عَنْ زَيْدِ بْنِ خَالِدٍ الْجُهَنِيّ قَالَ قَالَ رَسُولُ اللَّهِ ﷺ مَنْ فَطَّرَ صَائِمًا كَانَ لَهُ مِثْلُ أَجْرِهِمْ مِنْ غَيْرِ أَنْ يَنْقُصَ مِنْ أُجُورِهِمْ شَيْئًا

It was narrated from Zayd ibn Khālid al-Juhanī ﷺ that the Messenger of Allah ﷺ said: 'Whoever gives food for a fasting person to break his fast, he will have a reward like theirs, without that detracting from their reward in the slightest.'

Muslims are taught vital lessons through every act of worship. The primary lesson of worshipping Allah is to, of course, instil the concept of obedience to Allah and belief in His Oneness (*tawḥīd*). The secondary lesson is to create an awareness of our surroundings and inculcate compassion towards all of Allah's creation. It is not permissible for a Muslim to intentionally kill an ant for no reason. We may not understand it, but even ants play a very important part in maintaining the eco-system.

Worshipping Allah creates a sense of compassion within us towards those around us and makes us strive to attain betterment in society. Is it possible for a Muslim to pray the five daily prayers and not care about the well-being of their neighbours? Is it possible for a person to fast and not have compassion towards the poor? Is it possible that a person gives zakat money but pays no heed to the corruption in society? Is it possible for a person to perform hajj and not be concerned about social injustice? Therefore, worshipping Allah is not about empty rituals which are isolated from a broader purpose and higher objectives.

It is not the case that acts of worship have an identifiable aim and objective to which they are restricted. For example, the purpose of fasting is not restricted to teaching Muslims sympathy towards the poor and destitute, nor is hajj solely about racial harmony and unity. Rather, all acts of worship aim to improve the character of the worshipper to be a conscientious being who is aware of their surroundings, one who is conscious of Allah and strives to live the way He has guided us. This is called *taqwā*.

The primary aim of fasting is not to create awareness about the plight of the poor, though it may at times be a by-product of it. Every conscientious Muslim who fasts should feel the pain of hunger and spend some time to think about how the poor endure this pain every day continuously and not just during the daytime or only for a month. In order to encourage caring for each other, the Prophet ﷺ taught us that whoever gives food for a fasting person to break their fast will have a reward like theirs, without that detracting from their reward in the slightest. It is common that people always invite their friends and family over to break their fast together, but some attention needs to be paid to those who are less fortunate. In poor countries it is common for the poor and destitute to knock on the doors of the rich and ask for food to break their fasts. Feeding those people should be a priority without neglecting to invite your friends and family.

# Preparing for the Last Ten Days of Ramadan

عَنْ عَائِشَةَ قَالَتْ كَانَ النَّبِيُّ ﷺ إِذَا دَخَلَتِ الْعَشْرُ أَحْيَا اللَّيْلَ
وَشَدَّ الْمِئْزَرَ وَأَيْقَظَ أَهْلَهُ

It was narrated that 'Ā'ishah ﷻ said: 'When the last ten days of Ramadan began, the Prophet ﷺ used to stay up at night, tighten his waist-wrap, and wake up his family (to pray).'

The month of Ramadan is special for many reasons. It is the month in which Allah conferred the prophethood on Muhammad ﷺ and revealed the Qur'an to him. The month of Ramadan is packed with blessings and mercy. It is a month which Allah has filled with opportunities for salvation. In this month, Allah incarcerates Satan and rewards for every good deed in hundredfold multiples. There is a night in Ramadan which is equal to the worship of one thousand months—in fact, better than one thousand months!

The month of Ramadan is an opportunity for us to get closer to Allah, gain His forgiveness and have our prayers answered. It is a tough month because we cannot eat and drink as we do normally. This makes our daily lives more difficult. Going without food and water during the day and then spending the night worshipping Allah is hard, but the reward is well worth it. Imagine if by working one night you can earn the equivalent of one thousand months of work. Would anyone smart let that opportunity go?

The Prophet Muhammad ﷺ taught his followers the serious opportunity this month presents and in particular, the last ten days. The hadith tells us that he would 'tighten his waist-wrap', an expression to denote serious preparation. During the last ten days, when the Night of Power takes place, the Prophet ﷺ would stay awake in the worship of Allah and he would encourage his family members to do so too.

Every year the month of Ramadan repeats its offer, but there will be a time in everyone's life when they will live their last Ramadan. Before that time comes for us, let us seize the opportunities of Ramadan, especially the last ten days, and ask Allah for what we want, shed tears in hopes of forgiveness and try to seek out the Night of Power by exerting added effort and sincerity during all of the last ten nights of Ramadan.

৩৵৹

# 26

# Abuse of Authority

عَنِ ابْنِ عَبَّاسٍ أَنَّ النَّبِيَّ ﷺ بَعَثَ مُعَاذًا إِلَى الْيَمَنِ فَقَالَ إِنَّكَ
تَأْتِي قَوْمًا أَهْلَ كِتَابٍ فَادْعُهُمْ إِلَى شَهَادَةِ أَنْ لاَ إِلَهَ إِلاَّ اللهُ وَأَنِّي
رَسُولُ اللهِ فَإِنْ هُمْ أَطَاعُوا لِذَلِكَ فَأَعْلِمْهُمْ أَنَّ اللهَ افْتَرَضَ عَلَيْهِمْ
خَمْسَ صَلَوَاتٍ فِي كُلِّ يَوْمٍ وَلَيْلَةٍ فَإِنْ هُمْ أَطَاعُوا لِذَلِكَ فَأَعْلِمْهُمْ
أَنَّ اللهَ افْتَرَضَ عَلَيْهِمْ صَدَقَةً فِي أَمْوَالِهِمْ تُؤْخَذُ مِنْ أَغْنِيَائِهِمْ فَتُرَدُّ
فِي فُقَرَائِهِمْ فَإِنْ هُمْ أَطَاعُوا لِذَلِكَ فَإِيَّاكَ وَكَرَائِمَ أَمْوَالِهِمْ وَاتَّقِ دَعْوَةَ
الْمَظْلُومِ فَإِنَّهَا لَيْسَ بَيْنَهَا وَبَيْنَ اللهِ حِجَابٌ

Ibn ʿAbbās ؈ narrated that the Prophet ﷺ sent Muʿādh
to Yemen, and said: 'You are going to some people among
the People of the Book. Call them to bear witness that
none has the right to be worshipped but Allah, and that
I am the Messenger of Allah. If they obey that, then tell

them that Allah has enjoined upon them five prayers every day and night. If they obey that, then tell them that Allah has enjoined upon them zakat from their wealth, to be taken from the rich and given to their poor. If they obey that, then beware of (taking) the best of their wealth. And beware of the supplication of the oppressed, for there is no barrier between it and Allah.'

It is the duty of every Muslim to tell others about the message of Islam. The responsibility is to let them know of the main message of Islam, which is the call to the worship of One God, besides sharing with them the many other beautiful teachings of Islam. The propagation of Islam is done in a gentle manner with kindness and wisdom. This hadith teaches Muslims many valuable lessons such as the fundamentals of Islam that all Muslims must adhere to in order to show their loyalty to it and that they truly have submitted to the teachings of Islam and accept to worship Allah alone.

When Islam spread to new places the Prophet ﷺ would select a person from his Companions to teach them about Islam. He sent Mu'ādh ibn Jabal ﷺ to Yemen to tell the Jews and Christians over there about Islam. The Prophet ﷺ instructed Mu'ādh ﷺ to follow a particular method in his teaching. He told him to inform the Jews and Christians of Yemen to first, bear witness that none has the right to be worshipped but Allah, and that Muhammad is the Messenger of Allah. If they accepted this, the Prophet ﷺ told Mu'ādh ﷺ to then tell them about the five daily prayers which they must offer. If they accepted to do that, the Prophet Muhammad ﷺ told Mu'ādh ﷺ to tell them to give 2.5% of their wealth as zakat to the poor in their community.

Every human has an innate desire to possess wealth and money. This desire which is built into the fabric of human DNA means that we do not like to give up money, instead we like to hold on to it except when we give it up willingly either to buy something or we donate it as a gift or charity. We don't like it when we are forced to give money. No one likes to pay their taxes or fines. Although zakat is neither a tax nor a fine it is nevertheless taken from us whether we like it or not. Therefore, the Prophet ﷺ taught the zakat-collector an important message when taking zakat and that is not to take the best of a person's wealth. The Prophet ﷺ described this as an act of oppression and that the zakat-collector would be sinful and subject to curses from the person giving zakat. A person must not abuse their authority. This is the important message this hadith is trying to teach.

The hadith also teaches that zakat should be taken from the rich and given to the poor. This means that zakat should be distributed locally where possible. If there are no poor people in the local community or if the poor of other countries are in a much more desperate situation, then zakat can be given to them.

෴

# Can the Rich Take Zakat?

عَنْ أَبِي سَعِيدٍ الْخُدْرِيِّ قَالَ قَالَ رَسُولُ اللهِ ﷺ لاَ تَحِلُّ الصَّدَقَةُ
لِغَنِيٍّ إلاَّ لِخَمْسَةٍ لِعَامِلٍ عَلَيْهَا أَوْ لِغَازٍ فِي سَبِيلِ اللهِ أَوْ لِغَنِيٍّ
اشْتَرَاهَا بِمَالِهِ أَوْ فَقِيرٍ تُصُدِّقَ عَلَيْهِ فَأَهْدَاهَا لِغَنِيٍّ أَوْ غَارِمٍ

Abū Saʿīd al-Khudrī ﷺ narrated that the Messenger of
Allah ﷺ said: 'Zakat is not permissible for a rich man
except in five cases: One who is appointed to collect it,
a warrior fighting in the cause of Allah, a rich man who
buys it with his own money, a poor man who receives the
zakat and gives it as a gift to a rich man, and a debtor.'

Islam caters for everyone and seeks to secure the best interest for
all people. Islam pays particular interest to securing the rights of
the under-privileged, the poor, the weak and the vulnerable. This is
because these people usually do not have a voice and it is easy for those

stronger than them in status and power to abuse them or neglect their rights. The rules and codes of conduct in Islam are clear regarding the most vulnerable in the society. Neglecting those rules will make one sinful and answerable before Allah on the Day of Reckoning.

Those whom Allah has favoured with wealth and status should constantly bear in mind that what they have is from Allah and that it can be taken away from them at any time. So let them fear that Allah is watching them at all times. Although it might not be common, even the rich sometimes fall into hardship and need help. In Islam charity and zakat is primarily to help the poor and needy, but it has also made provisions for the rich in case they fall into hardship too. Zakat is also given to those involved in activities for the benefit of the wider community, such as fighters in war and those appointed to collect zakat.

This hadith teaches us the general rule that zakat is not permissible for the rich; it only belongs to the poor and needy. However, there *are* five circumstances in which the rich can access these funds. The first is a zakat-collector. This is a person employed by the State to go to businesses and individuals, work out their zakat and collect it. This is a fulltime job and it is very hard work. The zakat-collector may not be poor, but because it is their job to collect the zakat on behalf of the State, they are entitled to be paid from the money collected.

The second person is a member of the Muslim army. Every country needs armed forces that are dedicated to protecting the country from any hostile country or people. Army personnel need to be paid and everyone needs to contribute to paying for it. A portion of the zakat collected can be used by the State to pay army personnel, even if the soldier is rich.

What the Prophet Muhammad ﷺ meant by, 'a rich man who buys it with his own money' is that zakat can be either paid in cash, gold, silver or it can be paid in the actual item. For example, zakat is due on livestock such as sheep, cows, and camels. If a rich person wants to then buy an animal from a poor person who received that animal as zakat, they can do so, and thus take ownership of an item initially intended as zakat.

The fourth type is a poor person who receives the zakat, but he or she gives it as a gift to a rich person. If it is given as a gift, the rich person can accept it. Finally, it is possible that a rich person, thinking they will be able to get out of it, find themselves stuck in debt for some reason or another. For such people, zakat is available to help them get out of debt, get back into prosperity and once again be a zakat-giver rather than a zakat-receiver.

Through these teachings, Islam aims to look after everyone in society and strike a balance in order to meet the needs of the people.

# 28

# Four Reasons to Marry a Woman

عَنْ أَبِي هُرَيْرَةَ أَنَّ رَسُولَ اللَّهِ ﷺ قَالَ تُنْكَحُ النِّسَاءُ لِأَرْبَعٍ لِمَالِهَا وَلِحَسَبِهَا وَلِجَمَالِهَا وَلِدِينِهَا فَاظْفَرْ بِذَاتِ الدِّينِ تَرِبَتْ يَدَاكَ

It was narrated from Abū Hurayrah ﷺ that the Prophet ﷺ said: 'A woman is married for four things: Her wealth, her lineage, her beauty or for her religion. Choose the religious, may your hands be rubbed with dust (i.e., may you prosper).'

Allah created mankind to populate the earth and be the dominant inhabitants of it. He created us with specific needs and desires, one of them being the need for companionship and wanting to have a family. For that reason, Allah has ordained upon humanity the institution of marriage. Finding the right partner for marriage is not an easy task. There are many factors for consideration before people make a decision and as society changes, these factors increase in number.

Here the Prophet ﷺ has given advice to Muslim men regarding marriage. His first advice, recorded in another hadith, teaches us to give priority to religion and character over anything else. The Prophet ﷺ said to the guardians, 'If a person of good religion and character proposes marriage then marry them, for if you do not then there will be trials and tribulations upon Earth.'[14]

Putting the issue of character aside, the Prophet ﷺ said that a man seeks a woman in marriage for one of four reasons. If he marries her because of her wealth, that might bring him prosperity and financial assistance. Marrying into a good family helps a person move up the social ladder; so, a man may want to marry a woman from a good family for that reason. Beauty is the most popular reason for men to marry a woman. Men are easily enchanted by mere looks and for many men, beauty is the primary factor for marriage consideration, but the Prophet Muhammad ﷺ has taught us that one should marry a woman primarily for her religiosity.

There is another hadith which is not recorded with a strong chain of narrators, but it says, 'Do not marry women for their beauty for it may lead to their doom. Do not marry them for their wealth, for it may lead them to fall into sin. Rather, marry them for their religion.'

The Prophet ﷺ warned us about prioritising anything other than religious factors for marriage. Religion will guide the couple in their behaviour and conduct. There will be a day when a pretty woman may not be so attractive, and a rich woman may lose or exhaust her wealth. While everything may diminish, religiosity will continue to grow and strengthen people, and help towards building a righteous family.

Character and religiosity should be the two main factors for considerations when it comes to marriage. All other factors can also be considered. There is nothing wrong with seeking a beautiful wife. However, these other factors should be secondary.

---

14  Tirmidhi, *Jami' al-Tirmidhi*, Hadith no. 1084

# 29

# The Sin of Market Monopoly

عَنْ مَعْمَرِ بْنِ عَبْدِ اللَّهِ بْنِ عَبْدِ اللَّهِ بْنِ نَضْلَةَ قَالَ قَالَ رَسُولُ اللَّهِ ﷺ
لاَ يَحْتَكِرُ إِلاَّ خَاطِئٌ

It was narrated from Ma'mar ibn 'Abdullāh ibn Naḍlah ﷺ that the Messenger of Allah ﷺ said: 'No one hoards but a sinner.'

One of the key teachings of Islam is justice and fairness. The Prophet Muhammad's approach was always to look after the weak and vulnerable. This is because they are more likely to be abused and their rights are more likely to be violated. The Prophet ﷺ taught Muslims about social justice, roles and responsibilities. The burden of responsibility fell on the strong, the rich and the prosperous. Their privilege was not something they achieved without the help of Allah. The reason why some people are rich and others poor, why some are healthy and others ill, why some people are intelligent and others are not, is a secret of Allah. He gives people things in order to test them, to see whether they live up to their responsibilities. Do those who are privileged step up to their responsibilities and look after society's vulnerable members? The affluent in the society will have to face Allah and answer for this on the Day of Judgement.

One of the ways Allah will test people in their social responsibilities is in the way they behave during times of crisis. The rich always try to increase their wealth and the poor try to get themselves out of poverty. Getting rich and maintaining richness sometimes means that it is achieved on the backs of others. For those thinking about doing this, the Prophet ﷺ warned them of dire consequences. An example of this is monopolising the food market. That is to say, when the rich buy foodstuff in massive quantities and store it, thus stopping the supply of that product to the marketplace. The demand will rise and with it the price will too. Now that the demand is high, people are willing to pay very high prices for it. The foodstuff is then released to the market at a high price, leading to owners making a handsome profit off of it. The poorest in society are the ones who will suffer the most from this cycle which will inflict untold suffering on their already miserable lives.

In another hadith it is reported by Umar ibn al-Khaṭṭāb ﷺ that the Prophet Muhammad ﷺ said, 'Whoever hoards food (and keeps it from) the Muslims, Allah will afflict him with bankruptcy.'[15] The harm this behaviour has on society is extremely devastating and can spark civil unrest, fighting, and looting.

In modern times the same can apply to 'panic buying' where people who have money buy foodstuff and stock up their homes, because of news of some crisis. This puts pressure on shops and suppliers to maintain produce for people. The weakest and most vulnerable in society suffer when this happens which worsens the crisis. We must, at all times, behave sensibly and ethically, while keeping the welfare of others in mind.

---

15  Ibn Majah, *Sunan Ibn Majah*, Hadith no. 2155

# 30

# Code of Conduct during Trading

قَالَ عُثْمَانُ بْنُ عَفَّانَ قَالَ رَسُولُ اللَّهِ ﷺ أَدْخَلَ اللَّهُ رَجُلاً الْجَنَّةَ
كَانَ سَهْلاً بَائِعًا وَمُشْتَرِيًا

'Uthman ibn 'Affan ﷺ narrated that the Messenger of
Allah ﷺ said: 'Allah admitted to Paradise a man who was
lenient when he sold and when he bought.'

Allah has made trading lawful and a means by which people exchange ownership of things. Buying and selling are indispensable aspects of human life. It would be impossible for humans to live without it. This is because Allah has created humans as social creatures; they are limited in their ability to exist without the help of others. So, when humans live together, they become dependent on each other for their survival and without mutual cooperation life becomes extremely difficult. A person cannot be everything and do everything by himself or herself. For instance, a person cannot be a baker, teacher, builder, tailor and farmer all at the same time. So, a baker would need the help of a teacher to teach his or her children. A teacher cannot spend time in the fields growing rice so he or she needs the help of a farmer. A farmer cannot sew his or her own clothes so will need the help of a tailor. In this way, every person in society needs another person to make their life easier.

Buying and selling are a basic component of life and in the modern world we repeat this many times a day. It is a competitive part of life as it often occurs with the intention to make maximum profit. The zeal and eagerness to be successful in trading may cause some people to lose sight of the greater objective of trading, which is mutual cooperation and facilitating the existence of human life. During this engagement, feelings can be hurt. For example, people are always out there to get a bargain, and in the process of trying to secure a deal some people might make a ridiculous offer, or the seller may be aggressive to sell their product which may cause some people offense.

The Prophet Muhammad ﷺ taught his followers to be gentle, kind and understanding in trading. He told us that Allah will admit to Paradise those who are lenient when they sell and buy. This is indeed a great lesson, and it applies to everyone because at some stage everyone is either a buyer or a seller or both. Being gentle in trading is an easy way to gain the favour of Allah and secure a place in Paradise. In another hadith the Prophet ﷺ said, 'May Allah have mercy on a person who is lenient when he sells, lenient when he buys, and lenient when he asks for payment.'[16]

The story of the Prophet Muhammad ﷺ meeting his business partner is worth mentioning here. After the Conquest of Makkah, the Prophet's business partner, al-Sā'ib ibn Zayd al-Makhzumi came to meet him. The Prophet ﷺ greeted him with delight saying, 'Welcome to my brother, welcome to my partner.'[17] The Prophet ﷺ

---

16  Al-Bukhari, *Sahih al-Bukhari*, Hadith no. 2076

17  Abu Dawud, *Sunan Abu Dawud*, Hadith no. 4836

was delighted to meet him, because al-Sā'ib was a good man who was gentle in his character and manners in trading. He was an example of how to be a partner in business. Our behaviour and the way we deal with other people must be at a very high standard. Everyone likes to be treated with respect and kindness, so in order to receive the same, we must first show it. The Prophet ﷺ said, 'Treat people with the best character.'[18]

༺༻

---

18  Tirmidhi, *Jami' al-Tirmidhi*, Hadith no. 1987

# Taking Another Person's Property Wrongly

عَنْ أُمِّ سَلَمَةَ قَالَتْ قَالَ رَسُولُ اللهِ ﷺ إِنَّكُمْ تَخْتَصِمُونَ إِلَيَّ وَإِنَّمَا أَنَا بَشَرٌ وَلَعَلَّ بَعْضَكُمْ أَنْ يَكُونَ أَلْحَنَ بِحُجَّتِهِ مِنْ بَعْضٍ وَإِنَّمَا أَقْضِى بَيْنَكُمْ عَلَى نَحْوِ مِمَّا أَسْمَعُ مِنْكُمْ فَمَنْ قَضَيْتُ لَهُ مِنْ حَقِّ أَخِيهِ شَيْئًا فَلاَ يَأْخُذْهُ فَإِنَّمَا أَقْطَعُ لَهُ قِطْعَةً مِنَ النَّارِ يَأْتِي بِهَا يَوْمَ الْقِيَامَةِ

It was narrated from Umm Salamah ◉ that the Messenger of Allah ◉ said: 'You refer your disputes to me and I am only human. Perhaps some of you may be more eloquent in presenting your case than others, so I rule in your favour because of what I hear from you. If I pass a judgement in favour of one of you that detracts from his brother's rights, then he should not take it, because it is a

piece of fire that is given to him which he will bring forth
on the Day Resurrection.'

Gain with minimum effort is the holy grail of wealth. The thought of it is seductive and so appealing it is almost impossible to resist. Exploiting this human vulnerability are scam artists who dedicate their time and effort to cheat people by tricking them into thinking they will make a quick gain with little effort. People would part with their money in the false hope that they will receive a handsome windfall for minimum investment. The temptation to increase in wealth with minimum effort can also be by making a false claim to another person's property.

The law is all about trying to establish the truth, and this 'truth' must be established by evidence. However, the law can sometimes give or take from someone, due to the evidence provided, not necessarily because they are lawfully entitled to it, but because of the evidence provided. Human law must be based on evidence otherwise people would be taking the rights of others by merely making claims. The judge cannot be blamed at all if false evidence manufactured with the aim to seize another person's property is presented before them. The judge is duty-bound to decree according to the evidence. After all, the judge does not know who the property really belongs to and passes judgement only on the basis of the evidence provided and presented before them.

The Prophet Muhammad ﷺ warned his followers from pursuing the unethical path of providing false evidence to secure property. Sometimes evidence can be in the form of a persuasive argument. Not everyone has the ability to be convincing, and the Prophet ﷺ warned such people to beware of using articulation to falsely make claims.

In the modern world, we can see the legal profession where highly articulate lawyers would argue the case for their client, sometimes knowing that they are in the wrong, but nevertheless they would manipulate the law in order to win the case. This hadith serves as a warning to them as well as the person appointing the lawyer. The lawyer must be certain that the case they are fighting is sound and genuine. If they seek to exploit loopholes and secure the property of another person, they will share in this enormous sin and incur its punishment in the Hereafter.

# 32

# Stalling in Repaying Debt

عَنِ ابْنِ عُمَرَ قَالَ قَالَ رَسُولُ اللَّهِ ﷺ مَطْلُ الْغَنِيِّ ظُلْمٌ وَإِذَا
أُحِلْتَ عَلَى مَلِيءٍ فَاتْبَعْهُ

It was narrated from Ibn Umar ◌ that the Messenger of
Allah ◌ said: 'When a rich man takes too long to repay a
debt, this is wrongdoing; and if the debt is transferred to a
rich man, you should accept it.'

Not everyone has the resources in life to go without the need to
borrow money from others. Most of us will at some point in our
lives need to borrow money from friends and family. Although this
should be avoided as much as possible, sometimes there is no choice
but to borrow money. You will find even the rich who have millions
at their disposal borrow money in order to make investments and
business deals.

When taking a loan there are two very important factors to
consider. Firstly, the ability and means to pay it back; and secondly,

taking an amount within the means of a person. Islam encourages avoiding debt and taking loans. However, when it is not possible to refrain from borrowing, one may take a loan and then seek help from Allah to repay it. If they are sincere Allah will make a means to settle the debt.

There were certain things the Prophet ﷺ used to make constant prayer for, one of which was to be protected from being overcome with debt. Debt can have a massive impact on a person's mental well-being; therefore a person must take a loan only if they need it and if it is within their means to pay it back.

Once a person has the money to repay the debt they must do so without delay. Withholding repayment without any excuse is unethical in Islam. The Prophet Muhammad ﷺ described a person who has the money but delays repayment as a 'wrong-doer' or 'oppressor'. To show the seriousness of not paying back debts, the Prophet ﷺ once refused to pray the funeral prayer over someone who had not paid off his debts. Someone stood up and said, 'O Messenger of Allah I will repay his debt.' The Prophet ﷺ then stood and led his funeral prayer.[19] This is the seriousness of debt. This hadith clearly teaches us that when the money is available, the debt must be repaid immediately without any delay.

The second part of the hadith says that whenever one is referred to someone else capable of paying them, then they should go to that person to receive the money that they are owed. For example, if Ahmed owes Abdullah some money, and Khalid owes Ahmed the same amount or more, then Ahmed can send Abdullah to Khalid to collect his money. If Khalid is willing to pay, then Abdullah should accept this and not insist on receiving his money directly from Ahmed.

〄

---

19  Al-Bukhari, *Sahih al-Bukhari*, Hadith no. 2289

# 33

# *Guarantor of a Debt*

عن شُرَحْبِيلَ بْنُ مُسْلِمٍ الْخَوْلَانِيُّ قَالَ سَمِعْتُ أَبَا أُمَامَةَ الْبَاهِلِيَّ
يَقُولُ سَمِعْتُ رَسُولَ اللَّهِ ﷺ يَقُولُ الزَّعِيمُ غَارِمٌ وَالدَّيْنُ مَقْضِيٌّ

Shuraḥbīl ibn Muslim al-Khawlānī said: 'I heard Abū
Umāmah al-Bāhilī say: "I heard the Messenger of
Allah ﷺ say: 'The guarantor is responsible and the
debt must be repaid.'"'

Trust is an important part of a person's integrity. In order to
preserve one's integrity, a person must at all times maintain
their image as a trustworthy person. Remember, everyone is born
as a trustworthy person and no one is born as untrustworthy or
dishonest. These labels are attached to people later on in their lives
when they turn out to be either untrustworthy or dishonest. It is by
our reputation in society that people will deal with us in our personal
and business lives.

When it comes to matters related to money, it is natural that people need reassurance that the financial commitments will be honoured. Not everyone in society is the same, and it is not a matter of honesty or trustworthiness, rather a question of reassurance that when someone asks for a loan the lender may judge that they need some guarantor in case the borrower fails to repay the debt. This may be because the borrower may not be well-known to the lender or that the lender may believe that the borrower may falter in repayment due to the amount or the person's personal circumstance. The borrower may take a person to act as his or her guarantor or the lender may demand that the borrower brings a guarantor in case of defaulting on payment.

This hadith teaches Muslims a very important legal lesson. Firstly, it teaches us the permissibility of a person acting as a guarantor for another person. This is an optional element in transactions and it is not obligatory. If both parties agree to have a guarantor, then the guarantorship becomes obligatory. This hadith also teaches Muslims that once the guarantor agrees to the terms he or she cannot back out of the agreement. Rather, the debt in essence becomes the responsibility of the guarantor rather than the borrower. It is now the responsibility for the guarantor to ensure the repayment of the debt.

Islam has allowed guarantorship to help people. This is despite the principle in Islam that the burden or responsibility of one person cannot be transferred to another person. For example, if one person commits a crime another person cannot be punished in his place. Responsibility belongs to the person involved and cannot be passed on to another person even if they are willing to take it on. However, in financial matters Islam has shown a great deal of flexibility and has allowed others to take on the financial responsibility of others. This is to help facilitate human life and make difficult times easier.

# 34

# Being Easy with Debtors

عَنْ أَبِى هُرَيْرَةَ قَالَ قَالَ رَسُولُ اللَّهِ ﷺ مَنْ يَسَّرَ عَلَى مُعْسِرٍ يَسَّرَ
اللَّهُ عَلَيْهِ فِى الدُّنْيَا وَالْآخِرَةِ

It was narrated from Abū Hurayrah ☙ that the Messenger
of Allah ☙ said: 'Whoever is easy with (a debtor) who is in
difficulty, Allah will be easy with him in this world and in
the Hereafter.'

It is the Divine Will of Allah that He has created humans differently.
Not everyone is the same in intelligence, beauty, health, ability
and status. It is out of the wisdom of Allah that He chooses certain
people over others. Wealth is an easy example to see how Allah has
given millions to some people while others do not have a penny to
their names. The reason for this inequality is so that we may serve
each other. It is worth noting that everything in life is a test and as
such, everyone will be accountable. Allah says in the Qur'an: *'Allah
has raised you in rank some above others, so that He may test you in the
gifts He has given you'* (al-Anʿām 6: 165).

Money is an intrinsic commodity for human life. We need it to buy essential items in order to survive. The need to borrow money is a common feature in the lives of many and this is intensified by the fact that borrowing money is easier than repaying it. The poor constantly live in hardship and in most cases, they live their lives borrowing money on a day-to-day basis. In such circumstances, repaying debts can be extremely difficult. Hardship in repaying debt is not specific to the poor; it can also happen to those who are living more comfortably. The lenders may be anxious to get their money back and when the deadline has arrived and passed and no payment is received, they have the right to be upset and annoyed. They have the right to demand their money back and they have the right to take the person to court and force repayment by the court seizing their property and selling it to repay the lender. However, the Prophet Muhammad ﷺ encouraged people to be compassionate to those facing difficulties in repaying their debts. Islam tells us to be generous, give some time and even write it off if we can. Allah commands the Muslims in the Qur'an: *'If the debtor is in difficulty, grant him time till it is easy for him; but if you remit it by way of charity that is best for you, if you only knew'* (al-Baqarah 2: 280).

Although the Qur'an encourages writing the debt off, this may be difficult for many especially if the amount is significant. This hadith teaches us the reward of granting someone facing difficulties extra time or reducing their debt. Granting an extension is usually much easier because in most case lenders give money from the surplus money they have and so they will not need it straight way. Look at what the Prophet ﷺ promised those people who take pity upon the borrower and grant them an extension: 'Whoever is easy with (a debtor) who is in difficulty, Allah will be easy with him in this world and in the Hereafter.' This is a sure way to help ourselves on the Day of Judgement and ensure that Allah will be easy with us on that stressful day.

# 35

# The Rule of Law: Justice and Fairness for Everyone

عَنْ عَائِشَةَ أَنَّ قُرَيْشًا أَهَمَّهُمْ شَأْنُ الْمَرْأَةِ الْمَخْزُومِيَّةِ الَّتِي سَرَقَتْ فَقَالُوا مَنْ يُكَلِّمُ فِيهَا رَسُولَ اللَّهِ ﷺ قَالُوا وَمَنْ يَجْتَرِئُ عَلَيْهِ إِلاَّ أُسَامَةُ بْنُ زَيْدٍ حِبُّ رَسُولِ اللَّهِ ﷺ فَكَلَّمَهُ أُسَامَةُ فَقَالَ رَسُولُ اللَّهِ ﷺ أَتَشْفَعُ فِي حَدٍّ مِنْ حُدُودِ اللَّهِ ثُمَّ قَامَ فَاخْتَطَبَ فَقَالَ يَا أَيُّهَا النَّاسُ إِنَّمَا هَلَكَ الَّذِينَ مِنْ قَبْلِكُمْ أَنَّهُمْ كَانُوا إِذَا سَرَقَ فِيهِمُ الشَّرِيفُ تَرَكُوهُ وَإِذَا سَرَقَ فِيهِمُ الضَّعِيفُ أَقَامُوا عَلَيْهِ الْحَدَّ وَايْمُ اللَّهِ لَوْ أَنَّ فَاطِمَةَ بِنْتَ مُحَمَّدٍ سَرَقَتْ لَقَطَعْتُ يَدَهَا

It was narrated from 'Ā'ishah ﷺ that Quraysh became concerned about the case of the Makhzūmī woman who had stolen, and they said: 'Who will speak to the Messenger of Allah ﷺ concerning her?' They said: 'Who would dare to do that other than Usāmah ibn Zayd, the

beloved of the Messenger of Allah?' So Usāmah spoke
to him, and the Messenger of Allah 🕌 said, 'Are you
interceding concerning one of the legal limits of Allah?'
Then he stood up and addressed (the people) and said: 'O
people! Those who came before you were only destroyed
because when one of their nobles stole, they let him off,
but when one of the weak people among them stole, they
would carry out the punishment on him. By Allah, if
Fatima the daughter of Muhammad was to steal, I would
cut off her hand.'

Allah has commanded the faithful to follow His laws and implement them. The implementation of Allah's laws must be done without favour or prejudice. Everyone is equal before the law, not even the Prophets of Allah have exemption from it. Unfortunately, the practices of those from the past and present is that the rich and noble have special favours and privileges, and for them nothing is impossible because they have immunity from the law and they are usually above it. However, when it comes to the poor or people not of their social circle, the law is imposed without mercy and to the letter. There are many examples of this and its practice is evident without the need to mention particular cases, and unfortunately this problem still exists today in many countries.

During the time of the Prophet Muhammad 🕌 an incident took place where a noble woman was caught stealing. This was a scandal and highly embarrassing for the tribe of Banū Makhzūm. The members of the tribe wanted to conceal it and have her punishment dropped. They were fearful to approach the Prophet 🕌 with such a request so they decided to ask Usāmah ibn Zayd 🕌 to intercede on behalf of the woman. Usāmah ibn Zayd ﷺ was the son of Zayd ibn Ḥārithah ﷺ, and Zayd ibn Ḥārithah ﷺ was the adopted son of the Prophet Muhammad ﷺ. The Prophet ﷺ loved Zayd ibn Ḥārithah ﷺ like his own son, and he therefore saw Usāmah ibn Zayd like a grandson. The Prophet ﷺ loved Usāmah ibn Zayd so much, and it was because of the Prophet's love for him, the tribe of Banū Makhzūm thought their best chances lay with him.

Despite the deep love the Prophet ﷺ had for Usāmah ibn Zayd ﷺ, when he came to the Prophet ﷺ with such a proposal, he was not happy and told him sternly that the laws of Allah are not to be played with. The Prophet ﷺ does not have the authority to interfere with the laws of Allah or to apply them whenever he wishes. The Prophet ﷺ took this opportunity to warn Muslims of behaving in this way and said,

> 'O people! Those who came before you were only destroyed because when one of their nobles stole, they let him off; but when one of the weak people among them stole, they would carry out the punishment on him.'

To demonstrate his commitment to the rule of law, the Prophet ﷺ swore by Allah that even if his beloved daughter Fatima ﷺ were to steal she would not escape justice, and he would have most certainly cut her hand off.

༚ ۝ ༚

# 36

# Research, Experience and the Advice of the Prophet Muhammad ﷺ

عَنْ سِمَاكٍ أَنَّهُ سَمِعَ مُوسَى بْنَ طَلْحَةَ بْنِ عُبَيْدِ اللهِ يُحَدِّثُ

عَنْ أَبِيهِ قَالَ مَرَرْتُ مَعَ رَسُولِ اللهِ جَلَّوَعَلَا فِي نَخْلٍ فَرَأَى قَوْمًا

يُلَقِّحُونَ النَّخْلَ فَقَالَ مَا يَصْنَعُ هَؤُلَاءِ قَالُوا يَأْخُذُونَ مِنَ الذَّكَرِ

فَيَجْعَلُونَهُ فِي الْأُنْثَى قَالَ مَا أَظُنُّ ذَاكَ يُغْنِي شَيْئًا فَبَلَغَهُمْ

فَتَرَكُوهُ وَنَزَلُوا عَنْهَا فَبَلَغَ النَّبِيَّ جَلَّوَعَلَا فَقَالَ إِنَّمَا هُوَ ظَنٌّ إِنْ كَانَ

يُغْنِي شَيْئًا فَاصْنَعُوهُ فَإِنَّمَا أَنَا بَشَرٌ مِثْلُكُمْ وَإِنَّ الظَّنَّ يُخْطِئُ

وَيُصِيبُ وَلَكِنْ مَا قُلْتُ لَكُمْ قَالَ اللَّهُ فَلَنْ أَكْذِبَ عَلَى اللهِ

It was narrated from Simāk that he heard Mūsā ibn
Ṭalḥah ibn ʿUbaydullāh narrating that his father said:
ʿI passed by some palm trees with the Messenger of
Allah ﷺ and he saw some people pollinating the trees.
He said: "What are these people doing?" They said:

"They are taking something from the male part (of the plant) and putting it in the female part." He said: "I do not think that this will do any good." News of that reached them, so they stopped doing it, and their yield declined. News of that reached the Prophet ﷺ and he said: "That was only my thought. If it will do any good, then do it. I am only a human being like you, and what I think may be right or wrong. But when I tell you, 'Allah says...,' I will never tell lies about Allah.'"

Knowledge is what makes humans excel all other creations of Allah, and it is knowledge which makes one person excel over another. Allah says in the Qur'an: *'Say: Is the one who knows and the one who does not know the same?'* (*al-Zumar* 39: 9) What makes human knowledge special is their ability to do research by observation, investigation and experimentation. When we do that, we learn how things work. We understand the nature in which Allah has set creation to work and unravel its secrets. Once we have discovered this, we attempt to replicate it or work out how to get the best results from it. Through experience, trial and error, humans have learnt how to harvest and grow things, and for many centuries they have understood how to get the best produce. It is through trial and error that humans have learnt how much water is required for cultivation, when to sow the seeds and seedlings, and the like.

In Madinah, the Prophet ﷺ saw some people pollinating date trees and did not see any benefit in doing that, so he expressed his thoughts regarding it. Hearing his words, the farmers stopped doing it because they took the words of the Prophet ﷺ to be advice. Consequently, the dates yield reduced.

When the Prophet ﷺ heard of this he taught the Muslims a special lesson. He told them, 'Those were only my thoughts. If it will do any good, then do it. I am only a human being like you, and what I think may be right or wrong.' In other words, the words of the Prophet ﷺ regarding worldly matters such as agriculture, irrigation, baking or any other non-religious issues are not intended to be binding religious instructions. People are free to take them or not. This is because what the Prophet Muhammad ﷺ is expressing is his opinion based on experience or personal preference. It is not informed by Divine knowledge. However, if any religious instructions are given, then Muslims must obey them because these come from Allah.

# 37

# The Virtues of Bismillah before Eating

عَنْ عَائِشَةَ قَالَتْ كَانَ رَسُولُ اللَّهِ ﷺ يَأْكُلُ طَعَامًا فِى سِتَّةِ نَفَرٍ
مِنْ أَصْحَابِهِ فَجَاءَ أَعْرَابِيٌّ فَأَكَلَهُ بِلُقْمَتَيْنِ فَقَالَ رَسُولُ اللَّهِ ﷺ
أَمَا أَنَّهُ لَوْ كَانَ قَالَ بِسْمِ اللَّهِ لَكَفَاكُمْ فَإِذَا أَكَلَ أَحَدُكُمْ
طَعَامًا فَلْيَقُلْ بِسْمِ اللَّهِ فَإِنْ نَسِىَ أَنْ يَقُولَ بِسْمِ اللَّهِ فِى أَوَّلِهِ
فَلْيَقُلْ بِسْمِ اللَّهِ فِى أَوَّلِهِ وَآخِرِهِ

It was narrated that 'Ā'ishah ❀ said: 'The Messenger of
Allah ﷺ was eating food with six of his Companions
when a Bedouin came and ate it all in two bites. The
Messenger of Allah ﷺ said: "If he had said *bismillah* (In
the name of Allah), it would have sufficed you (all). When
any one of you eats food, let him say *bismillah*, and if
he forgets to say *bismillah* at the beginning, let him say:

## *Bismillāh fī awwalihi wa ākhirihi* (In the Name of Allah at the beginning and at the end).'"

It is often not a question of how much you have, but a question of whether what you have serves you best. This phenomenon can only occur because of *barakah* or blessing from Allah Most High. There are some people who earn thousands of pounds a month but at the end of the month they have little to nothing to show for it. There are people who have millions, yet they do not feel satisfied and content with what they have. This is because the *barakah* from Allah is missing. This is why you will see some people who have little money scraping by, yet they are happy with what they have, it suffices them and they live a satisfied life.

It is the blessing of Allah that makes what you have serve you to the fullest. Have you ever felt unsatisfied after having eaten a plate full of food? Well, in this hadith the Prophet Muhammad ﷺ has shed some light on it and taught his followers how blessings are attained in food and eating. Once a Bedouin man came to Madinah for a visit. The Prophet Muhammad ﷺ was sitting and eating with his Companions. It was the custom of the Arabs and the Sunnah of the Prophet ﷺ to eat in a shared plate. While they were enjoying their food, the Bedouin sat and joined in, and he managed to eat the contents of the plate in a few bites. Neither the Prophet ﷺ nor the Companions got annoyed with the man, but the Prophet ﷺ remarked, 'If he had said *bismillah*, it would have sufficed all of you.' In other words, by not saying '*bismillah*' the blessings of Allah were taken away, otherwise, the little food they were enjoying would have sufficed them all.

Then the Prophet ﷺ imparted another very important lesson to his Companions. He taught them that they should say *bismillah* before eating and if they forget to say it, they should say, '*bismillāh fī awwalihi wa ākhirihi*'. A person should say this as soon as they remember. When we say this, Allah will place *barakah* in our food, make even a little amount satisfying for us, make the food beneficial for our body and prevent harm from afflicting it.

So, it is not a matter of how much you have eaten, but *how* you have eaten that food. If you have recited '*bismillah*', you are showing gratefulness to Allah. It shows that you have recognised that Allah has provided you with this food, that you are mindful of Allah and that you seek only His blessings.

෴

# 38

# Eating in Moderation and Avoiding Overeating

يَقُولُ الْمِقْدَامَ بْنَ مَعْدِيكَرِبَ سَمِعْتُ رَسُولَ اللّهِ ﷺ يَقُولُ مَا
مَلأَ آدَمِيٌّ وِعَاءً شَرًّا مِنْ بَطْنٍ حَسْبُ الآدَمِيّ لُقَيْمَاتٌ يُقِمْنَ
صُلْبَهُ فَإِنْ غَلَبَتِ الآدَمِيَّ نَفْسُهُ فَثُلُثٌ لِلطَّعَامِ وَثُلُثٌ لِلشَّرَابِ
وَثُلُثٌ لِلنَّفَسِ

Miqdām ibn Ma'dīkarib ⬟ said: 'I heard the Messenger of Allah ⬟ say: "A human being fills no vessel worse than his stomach. It is sufficient for a human being to eat a few mouthfuls to keep his spine straight, but if he must (fill it), then one-third for food, one-third for drink and one-third for breathing."'

E ating is a social experience for humans and one of the most vital things for our survival. From the time we wake up to the time we sleep, we engage in eating throughout the day whether that is in the form of snacks, drinks or a full meal. Eating is a pleasurable experience and humans are always on the quest to explore ways of making food more delicious. People pay a lot of money to eat food prepared by expert cooks and sometimes travel many miles for that experience.

Unfortunately, in the modern world especially, we can see the adverse effects of overeating. Because the production and availability of food is greater than ever before, the temptation to eat and indulge is greater than ever before. As a result, we know that in societies where overeating is prevalent, there is an obesity crisis and people face massive health problems. In fact, many health problems are a direct result of what we consume as food. Just as what we eat matters, so does how much we eat of it. Overeating puts stress on the body and the organs to deal with the excessive food. Over the process of many years, this has terrible consequences on health such as increased blood pressure, cholesterol, blood sugar levels and other things.

This hadith is an amazing insight into the guidance the Prophet Muhammad ﷺ provided Muslims regarding dietary portions. Sticking by those guidelines will ensure good health until old age. Firstly, the Prophet ﷺ warns that, 'a human being fills no vessel worse than his stomach.' This is because it is a source of ill-health and creates a habit of greed and lack of discipline. He then tells us that 'it is sufficient for a human being to eat a few mouthfuls to keep his spine straight,' so that we can survive and remain healthy enough to function well throughout the day. However, this is very difficult to uphold all the time for the vast majority of us, and it is natural for us to crave for more food. So, the Prophet ﷺ told us that if someone does want to eat more, they should conceptually divide their stomach into three parts: one-third for food, one-third for drink and one-third for breathing. The adult stomach is about 12 inches long and 6 inches wide; if that is divided into three it is easy to estimate how much we should be eating.

The Prophet Muhammad ﷺ was never described as having a protruding tummy. Rather his belly was flat which suggests the Prophet ﷺ never overate nor was it his habit to do so. This teaching falls in line with his teaching of moderation and balance. Acting upon this hadith will ensure good health and enjoying all types of healthy and delicious food without restriction even into old age.

෴

# 39

# The Wrong Way to Sleep

عَنْ قَيْسِ بْنِ طِخْفَةَ الْغِفَارِيّ عَنْ أَبِيهِ قَالَ أَصَابَنِي رَسُولُ اللَّهِ
ﷺ نَائِمًا فِي الْمَسْجِدِ عَلَى بَطْنِي فَرَكَضَنِي بِرِجْلِهِ وَقَالَ مَا لَكَ
وَلِهَذَا النَّوْمِ هَذِهِ نَوْمَةٌ يَكْرَهُهَا اللَّهُ أَوْ يُبْغِضُهَا اللَّهُ

It was narrated from Qays ibn Ṭikhfah al-Ghifārī that his
father said: 'The Messenger of Allah ﷺ found me sleeping
in the *masjid* on my stomach. He nudged me with his foot
and said: "Why are you sleeping like this? This is a kind of
sleep that Allah dislikes, or that Allah hates."'

Although Allah has created humans in a unique way, He has
nevertheless created us with many weaknesses. Our weaknesses
are due to our finite existence on Earth, and in certain traits when
compared to other creations like the angels and jinns. Although
humans may surpass angels and jinns in knowledge, humans are
however, considerably physiologically deficient in comparison to

them. Our ability to endure the elements is limited and we suffer from many issues which make us vulnerable. Allah has given humans the ability to figure out ways of survival and to work our way around surviving those weaknesses. One of our human weaknesses is that we tire quite easily. Our bodies sustain small, microscopic damages during the course of our work every day. Allah has given humans sleep in order to help us recover from tiredness and help the body repair damages.

Sleep is a wonderful thing and it is a mystery how we fall asleep and what happens to our consciousness during sleep. During the time of sleep, it is as if our souls have left our bodies and we become lifeless. It does not matter how tired we are, a good night's sleep helps us 'recharge' and regain strength to carry on the next day. Imagine what would happen if we could not sleep? It would cause great difficulties and discomfort and shorten our lives.

In Islam, the Prophet Muhammad ﷺ taught us the etiquette of sleep. It is recommended for a person to sleep in the state of ablution (*wuḍū*). One should lie facing their right side and recite the supplications for sleep taught by the Prophet ﷺ, such as, '*Allāhumma bismika amūtu wa aḥyā*'.

In this hadith the Prophet ﷺ taught Muslims how *not* to sleep. Ṭikhfah al-Ghifārī ﷺ was once sleeping tummy side down. The Prophet ﷺ saw him and woke him up and told him not to sleep like this, because Allah does not like sleep in this fashion. Tikhfah al-Ghifārī ﷺ could not remember if the Prophet ﷺ said that Allah dislikes that style of sleep or hates it; either way, the words indicate that it is better to not sleep on your stomach.

As such, it is a duty of all Muslims to avoid sleeping like that. It is worth noting that the hadith is not talking about a person turning on his tummy during the stupor of sleep unconsciously, but it is talking about lying down on the tummy preparing for sleep and then falling asleep in that position. That is what is disliked.

# Asking Allah for Jannah

عَنْ أَنَسِ بْنِ مَالِكٍ قَالَ قَالَ رَسُولُ اللهِ ﷺ مَنْ سَأَلَ الْجَنَّةَ ثَلاَثَ
مَرَّاتٍ قَالَتِ الْجَنَّةُ اللَّهُمَّ أَدْخِلْهُ الْجَنَّةَ وَمَنِ اسْتَجَارَ مِنَ النَّارِ
ثَلاَثَ مَرَّاتٍ قَالَتِ النَّارُ اللَّهُمَّ أَجِرْهُ مِنَ النَّارِ

It was narrated from Anas ibn Mālik ﷺ that the
Messenger of Allah ﷺ said: 'Whoever asks for Paradise,
three times, Paradise will say: "O Allah, admit him to
Paradise." And whoever asked to be saved from Hell, three
times, Hell will say: "O Allah, save him from Hell."'

The purpose of human creation is to worship Allah and by
worshipping Allah humans will be granted the ultimate
reward, Jannah. Jannah is the Arabic word for Paradise. It is the
place Allah has created with unimaginable beauty, comfort and joy.
No one can imagine Jannah because the Prophet Muhammad ﷺ

told us that our minds cannot conceive the beauty and splendour of it. Its luxury is indescribable and the joy therein is unimaginable.

In Jannah people will be free to do what they want. Allah will remove all evil from the hearts so there will be no jealousy, no greed, no fighting or any type of ill feelings for others. There is nothing but peace and comfort; boredom will not exist and every day will bring renewed pleasure.

No one will feel hunger and thirst, but people will eat and drink for pleasure, and unlike this world, in Jannah there will be no adverse effects to eating. There will be no illness, no old age and no poverty. Whatever the people of Jannah want, they simply need to think about it and desire for it to be presented to them. There will be rivers flowing, meetings and greetings and untold merriment. This is the reward for those who make sacrifices in this life and choose to obey Allah and His Messenger ﷺ.

Jannah is the original home for us, humans. Attaining it is easy if one seeks Allah's help and does their utmost best. All we have to do is obey Allah by praying five times a day, paying our zakat, fasting the month of Ramadan and going to hajj if we can afford it. We must avoid the things Allah has made forbidden for us such as worshipping anything other than Allah, murder, cheating, drinking alcohol, illicit relationships and other major sins. If we happen to commit sins, then we should immediately seek Allah's forgiveness and reform our behaviour so that our sins are erased.

The reason why you are reading this book of hadith is for the sake of knowledge, so you can learn about Allah and His religion with the hope that through knowledge you can get closer to Allah and by getting closer to Allah you can get Jannah. The Prophet ﷺ taught us that the path of learning knowledge is a path to Jannah.

In this hadith, the Prophet ﷺ taught us to ask Allah for Jannah and to ask Him to save us from Hell. We should make this supplication regularly, because it shows that our desire for Jannah is genuine, and this will then encourage us to act to attain it. The ultimate goal in this life is to worship Allah and get Jannah. You can make this supplication in Arabic by saying, *'Allāhumma adkhil-ni'l jannah'* and seek refuge in Allah from Hell by saying, *'Allāhumma ajir-nī min an-nār,'* or you can say it in any language that you find easy.

May Allah grant us Jannah and save us from the Hellfire. *Āmīn.*